Praise for *Making Every MFL Lesson Count*

Making Every MFL Lesson Count is a thoroughly enjoyable read. It is honest, informative, rooted in research and shares ideas that are applicable to everyday MFL lessons.

Kate Carter, Head of MFL, Winstanley School

When I heard that there was an MFL edition in the Making Every Lesson Count series, I was really excited – and upon reading it I was really pleased to see that James has stayed true to the format of the original book, while acknowledging that MFL teaching and learning varies from that of other subjects in a number of ways.

The mini case studies really help to set the scene at the start of each chapter, and the reflective questions are not only useful for personal reflection but also serve as helpful prompts for departmental meetings and development planning. What is also pleasing is the healthy balance that James has struck between references to research and his offering of a range of strategies that can be applied and adapted in the classroom. James also takes care to acknowledge the difficulties educators face in MFL teaching, such as time constraints, and factors these into his suggestions.

Making Every MFL Lesson Count will be useful for any MFL teacher; I'll most definitely be recommending it to my colleagues. I'm certain it will shape my thinking when it comes to my planning, both of the curriculum and my individual lessons.

Rebecca Nobes, Head of Spanish, The Boswells School, and member of the Chartered College of Teaching Council

Making Every MFL Lesson Count is a timely resource for MFL teachers and heads of department. Timely, as it is based on the belief that languages are increasingly important in order to maintain positive attitudes and behaviours across our global society, but also because it is rooted in some of the latest research on what works in the classroom – particularly in terms of pedagogy and cognitive science, with particular links to memory. The balance between theory and practice is great and this, in my opinion, makes Maxwell's work an essential read.

Dr Sebastien Chapleau, Head Teacher, La Fontaine Academy

Making every
MFL
lesson count

*Six principles to support
modern foreign language teaching*

James A. Maxwell

Edited by Shaun Allison and Andy Tharby

Crown House Publishing Limited
www.crownhouse.co.uk

First published by

Crown House Publishing Limited
Crown Buildings, Bancyfelin, Carmarthen, Wales, SA33 5ND, UK
www.crownhouse.co.uk

and

Crown House Publishing Company LLC
PO Box 2223, Williston, VT 05495, USA
www.crownhousepublishing.com

British Library Cataloguing-in-Publication Data

A catalogue entry for this book is available from the British Library.

Print ISBN 978-178583396-0
Mobi ISBN 978-178583479-0
ePub ISBN 978-178583480-6
ePDF ISBN 978-178583481-3

LCCN 2019953052

Printed and bound in the UK by
TJ International, Padstow, Cornwall

Contents

Acknowledgements

I would like to thank Shaun Allison and Andy Tharby for writing the original book that began this series. It had a big impact on both my teaching and, by extension, the approach to teaching and learning in the school where I was principal. I also wish to thank other members of the extended Making Every Lesson Count family – notably Mark Enser, Emma McCrea, Jo Payne, Mel Scott and Chris Runeckles – for their inspiration.

My appreciation goes to the amazing MFL departments at Markethill High School and Carrickfergus Grammar School. Their undiluted and unceasing joy and enthusiasm for the teaching of modern foreign languages reminds me always of the privilege and importance of teaching children a second language. Special thanks to Faith McMullan-Ramirez, head of MFL at Markethill High School, who gave incredible support to me while I was writing this book. Thank you also to Michelle McAllister and Begoña Claver for their support with translations – both outstanding teachers of MFL.

On a personal level, I extend my deepest gratitude to those who have inspired me over many years in education. This includes my first ever teacher of German, Elisabeth Conn, who gave me a love of language learning; my first head of department, Alan Wilson, one of the most brilliant French teachers I have had the privilege of working with; and Wilbert Hollinger, former vice principal of Ballyclare High School and the biggest influence on my career to date.

Finally, I would like to thank my parents, Ann and Mo, who instilled in me the value of education and a strong work ethic, and who sacrificed much to make sure my brother Ian and I got the best education possible. Thank you for your support, patience and example.

Introduction

To have another language is to possess a second soul.

Attributed to Charlemagne

As someone who lives and works in Northern Ireland, approximately thirty miles from the border with the Republic of Ireland, the reverberations of Brexit are significant and acute. However, alongside many other pertinent debates, Brexit has reignited the discussion about the importance of foreign language learning and given it a new dynamic. This discussion should give us all, from the government down, the opportunity to dispel once and for all the myth that we sometimes hear from our more reticent students – and sadly from too many adults – that the predominance of English negates the need to learn a foreign language.

The evidence to the contrary is incontrovertible, as documented in the British Council's 2017 publication *Languages for the Future*.[1] In a constantly shifting globalised economy

---

1   British Council, *Languages for the Future: The Foreign Languages the United Kingdom Needs to Become a Truly Global Nation* (2017). Available at: https://www.britishcouncil.org/sites/default/files/languages_for_the_future_2017.pdf.

there is no such thing as a static lingua franca. Willy Brandt, the former German chancellor, once said: "If I am selling to you, I speak your language. If I am buying, *dann müssen Sie Deutsch sprechen.*"[2]

The impact of language skills deficiencies in the UK had already been widely reported well before the 2016 referendum. A UK Trade and Investment commissioned review from 2014 suggests that the economy is losing £48 billion per year, or 3.5% of GDP, in lost contracts due to a strong language barrier and lack of language skills in the workplace.[3]

In a post-Brexit landscape, with the potential requirement for hundreds of new and robust trade deals, it is very likely that foreign language learning will be of huge importance to future prospects. It may also avoid costly and embarrassing translation errors and possible cross-cultural offence. Perhaps one of the most notable examples of this was when American Motors launched its Matador car in Puerto Rico, despite 'Matador' meaning 'killer' in Spanish!

---

2 Quoted in Aida Edemariam, Who Still Wants to Learn Languages?, *The Guardian* (24 August 2010). Available at: https://www.theguardian.com/education/2010/aug/24/who-still-wants-learn-languages.

3 James Foreman-Peck and Yi Wang, *The Costs to the UK of Language Deficiencies as a Barrier to UK Engagement in Exporting: A Report to UK Trade and Investment* (Cardiff: Cardiff Business School, 2014), p. 35. Available at: https://www.gov.uk/government/publications/the-costs-to-the-uk-of-language-deficiencies-as-a-barrier-to-uk-engagement-in-exporting.

As MFL teachers, we are well aware of the vital role foreign language skills can play in the workplace, and not just for business. We do not need to be persuaded that the promotion of language learning should be a top priority for governments. Yet we also know that language learning is much more than a useful practical skill; it brings with it immense emotional, intellectual, cultural, social and personal benefits. It kindles an awareness of and opens doors to some of the world's greatest writers, thinkers, scientists, musicians and philosophers. It also teaches us about ourselves, our own language, values and culture. As the great German writer Goethe once said: "He who does not speak foreign languages knows nothing about his own."

Writing in *The Observer* in July 2017, British author John le Carré described the importance of language learning as an act of friendship and a route to negotiation.[4] In his musings on why he loves the German language and what drove him to go to university in Switzerland, and later to teach German at Eton College, he pins it down to one core reason: the excellence of his teacher. He recalls with fondness the gramophone records which his teacher cherished deeply and which he kept in brown paper bags in a satchel placed in his bicycle basket on the way to school. Those gramophone records, which were quite a novelty to English public schoolboys of the 1940s, contained the voices of classical German actors reciting German poetry. Le Carré recounts how he himself learnt this poetry by heart, which was made even more meaningful, unique and memorable by the frequent cracks of the gramophone records. Above all, he paints the picture of a teacher who (despite much anti-German sentiment and propaganda at the time) resolutely endeavoured to convey his passion for language – its beauty, accuracy and meaning within a cultural and literary framework.

---

4   John le Carré, Why We Should Learn German, *The Observer* (2 July 2017). Available at: https://www.theguardian.com/education/2017/jul/02/ why-we-should-learn-german-john-le-carre.

While the context of our own educational backgrounds may be very different to that of le Carré's, many of us will no doubt remember with fondness a teacher who inspired us. If you are an MFL teacher, there is a strong chance that the teacher you are thinking of taught languages. If we were to undertake a straw poll of why they inspired us, popular answers might include their passion for the language, their expert knowledge of the subject, their enthusiasm and encouragement, how they guided our journey from complete beginner to advanced linguist, the cultural anecdotes that peppered their lessons and gave flavour to the learning context, or how they made the language meaningful and relevant within the confines of a school classroom.

Teaching a modern foreign language is a real joy. I work as a teaching principal. I love nothing more than being able to close the door of my classroom and teach my discipline. I love the sense of excitement of Year 7 students, many of whom have not encountered the language to any great extent previously, as they come to grips with its rudimentary aspects. I love the sense of fun that we can have with language. Who could imagine that the nearest translation for 'hen-pecked husband' in German is *Pantoffelheld* (literally 'slipper hero'!)? Who could fail to be impressed that the Germans actually have a word for someone who takes the path of least resistance in life – *Dünnbrettbohrer* (literally 'driller of thin boards'!)? I love the potential which MFL teachers have to mould a student's language learning journey and, if we get the curriculum design right, to see the cumulative development of that learning journey unfold over time through the schema of linguistic knowledge which they build in their long-term memory. I love the sense of achievement in students' eyes when they are able to negotiate meaning successfully and sustain communication as a result.

To illustrate this anecdotally, I remember taking a school trip to Germany some years ago. It is a true pleasure to observe students immerse themselves in the language and culture of the target language country. One Year 9 student was making a purchase in a large department store, when the sales assistant asked her 'Sammeln Sie Flugmeilen?' (Do you collect air miles?) – not exactly the most obvious question you would expect to be asked when making a purchase. I was on the cusp of stepping in to assist the student after witnessing the fleeting look of panic on her face. However, by the time I reached her, she had already responded 'Nein' to the gentleman behind the counter and was able to advise me that she was being asked if she collected air miles. I was impressed because air miles had not featured anywhere on the curriculum. When I asked her how she knew, she told me that she had picked up the word 'Flug' from the flight to Germany three days earlier, and 'Meilen' sounded like 'miles' in English. She knew the verb 'sammeln' from curriculum study in Year 8 on 'hobbies and leisure'. She was quite chuffed at her achievement, as was I!

As teachers of modern foreign languages, we have a huge responsibility. In 'Making the Case for the Future of Languages', Rosamond Mitchell defines the instrumental and integrative reasons for the importance of language learning and teaching.[5] She observes that in an era of globalisation, no global language system is static. Chinese, Spanish and Hindi are identified alongside other 'supercentral' languages, such as French, Russian and German, as potential contenders to displace English in key regions of world economic activity. Moreover, at ages 11–16 in particular, language learning makes a vital contribution to the development of students' metalinguistic understanding, enabling them to draw consistent comparisons between their first language and the target language, thus developing their practical control of the target language.

Language learning also allows for the development of intercultural understanding and competence as well as a

---

5   Rosamond Mitchell, Making the Case for the Future of Languages. In Patricia
    Driscoll, Ernesto Macaro and Ann Swarbrick (eds), *Debates in Modern
    Languages Education* (Abingdon: Routledge, 2013), pp. 203–217.

broadening of students' communicative repertoire. By teaching modern foreign languages, we are ultimately giving our students the knowledge, skills and aptitudes which may help them to live productive, successful and fulfilled lives. The very first sentence of the Department for Education's national curriculum for language study in England states: "Learning a foreign language is a liberation from insularity and provides an opening to other cultures."[6]

Nobody could claim to have come up with an ideal method to teach modern foreign languages. Many MFL classrooms may subscribe to communicative language teaching (CLT), a broad functional approach based on the recognition that students need to develop the ability to communicate in the target language, and not just possess a passive knowledge of vocabulary, structure and grammar rules. Indeed, exam specifications and national curriculum guidelines reflect this, highlighting the need for communicative input in the form of listening and reading as well as modified output from the student through spoken and written means. In other words, students need to receive and comprehend information which is communicated to them and communicate effectively in the target language, often as a response to input.

However, as Elspeth Broady discusses in 'Foreign Language Teaching: Understanding Approaches, Making Choices', CLT has been associated with a lot of misunderstanding.[7] In the 1990s and 2000s, it was assumed by many that CLT required the target language to be used at all times in the classroom, that grammar in particular was not explicitly taught but rather 'inferred', and that formal grammar and error correction should be banished as it might undermine the development of target language skills. Indeed, during

---

6   See https://www.gov.uk/government/publications/national-curriculum-in-england-languages-progammes-of-study/national-curriculum-in-england-languages-progammes-of-study#key-stage-3-modern-foreign-language.

7   Elspeth Broady, Foreign Language Teaching: Understanding Approaches, Making Choices. In Norbert Pachler and Ana Redondo (eds), *A Practical Guide to Teaching Foreign Languages in the Secondary School*, 2nd edn (Abingdon: Routledge, 2014), pp. 1–10.

my own initial teacher training in the late 1990s, the use of English in the classroom was frowned upon. Students were encouraged to work grammar rules out for themselves – the 'inductive approach'. What took thirty minutes for them to infer could probably have been explained to them explicitly in ten minutes, and the remaining time used for modelling and deliberate practice. As a result, at times during my early years of teaching it felt as if I was playing a game of 'guess what's in the teacher's head' with my students. This, coupled with a centralised curriculum which prioritised so-called generic and/or transferable skills such as working with others and problem-solving, sometimes made me feel as if my expertise as a linguist was somewhat redundant in the classroom.

More recent research has pointed to the significant role which the explicit learning of language forms can play in developing language ability. For example, Robert DeKeyser gives an overview of how explicit knowledge of the target grammatical element may ultimately be converted into proceduralised knowledge.[8] This means that with practice the knowledge gradually becomes automatic, and the user of the language (whether spoken or written) no longer has to think about the rules or the pattern – it just comes out. In a complementary manner, the Teaching Schools Council's *Modern Foreign Languages Pedagogy Review* in 2016 states:

An explicit but succinct description of the grammatical feature to be taught, its use/meaning/function, and where appropriate a comparison with English usage (eg when the new language differs in complex ways to English) is conducive to correctly and efficiently understanding the function and meaning of grammar. There is evidence that waiting for pupils to identify grammatical patterns, without prompting them to do so, is not

---

8   Robert DeKeyser, Skill Acquisition Theory. In Bill VanPatten and Jessica
    Williams (eds), *Theories in Second Language Acquisition: An Introduction*
    (Mahwah, NJ: Erlbaum, 2006), pp. 94–112.

usually conducive to effective learning, particularly for complex or unfamiliar structures.[9]

Not unrelated, perhaps, is research which suggests that judicious use of students' first language in MFL classrooms can be facilitative of learning rather than an obstacle. Broady expounds on this by discussing how most of us will instinctively link and check new words and expressions we have learnt in the target language back to our first language.[10] This not only develops and consolidates our target language knowledge, but also builds our knowledge about language in general and, as a consequence, our metalinguistic skills, notably our ability to reflect on oral and written language and how it is used.

The skill of translating from the target language into our first language is in itself a real communicative skill. Not only is this now emphasised at an earlier stage through its inclusion in the new GCSE specifications, but our students at age 16 also have to answer comprehension questions in their first language on MFL listening and reading papers and infer meaning from what they hear and read. While not taking a stance on the target language debate, this book assumes that most MFL teachers may indeed be using the students' first language judiciously in the classroom as part of their teaching approaches, while not neglecting, of course, the huge importance of strong exposure to the target language in order to exploit natural acquisition mechanisms.

In 2014, the Sutton Trust produced a report which reviewed over 200 pieces of research and consequently argued that many things which are considered popular teaching

---

9 Ian Bauckham, *Modern Foreign Languages Pedagogy Review: A Review of Modern Foreign Languages Teaching Practice in Key Stage 3 and Key Stage 4* (Teaching Schools Council) (2016), p. 10. Available at: https://www.tscouncil.org.uk/wp-content/uploads/2016/12/MFL-Pedagogy-Review-Report-2.pdf.
10 Broady, Foreign Language Teaching, p. 11.

practices are, in fact, ineffective.[11] These include encouraging students to discover ideas for themselves, attempting to improve motivation before teaching content, teaching to what many now consider to be mythical 'learning styles' and the idea that active learning helps you to remember. Conversely, the report also highlighted two factors which are considered to link most acutely to the strongest student outcomes:

- ♦ **Content knowledge:** Teachers with strong knowledge and understanding of their subject make a greater impact on students' learning.

- ♦ **Quality of instruction:** This includes effective questioning and use of assessment by teachers. Also shown to be important are practices including reviewing previous learning, providing model responses for students, scaffolding new learning and giving students adequate time to practise and embed knowledge securely.[12]

The Sutton Trust report, alongside other research that we will encounter in this book, undoubtedly provides a strong foundation to validate the decisions we make about our approaches to planning, learning, teaching and assessment in our classrooms. One of the main goals of this book is to synthesise the latest research on teaching and learning and to explore how it applies to the MFL classroom.

However, as MFL teachers we know very well that we often need to apply a unique filter when examining how the best research can be translated for our subject. Effective questioning in the MFL classroom, for example, looks very different from that in the history classroom up the corridor where questioning is being undertaken in the students' first language. Explanation in the MFL classroom is a much different beast from the exposition being given by the science

---

11 Robert Coe, Cesare Aloisi, Steve Higgins and Lee Elliot Major, *What Makes Great Teaching? Review of the Underpinning Research* (London: Sutton Trust, 2014). Available at: https://www.suttontrust.com/research-paper/great-teaching.

12 Coe et al., *What Makes Great Teaching?*, pp. 2–3.

teacher on the floor above. Anecdotes in the MFL classroom may have a different dynamic and purpose than those employed in other subjects. Therefore, alongside a close analysis of general cognitive research, it would be foolish not to place value on what second-language acquisition research tells us.

We should also pay heed to the practical wisdom of classroom teachers who, over many years and often through trial and error, have teased out what works best and what teaching skills are most effective in the many differing contexts of the MFL classroom. For example, my own experience as an MFL teacher of twenty years' standing has instinctively led me to the conviction that, alongside strong subject knowledge, one of the most effective skills as a teacher is the ability to identify where student misconceptions are likely to occur, to plan lessons accordingly and – if misconceptions ultimately do arise – to address them skilfully in the classroom. This may not be rocket science, but experience has taught me that it can have a big impact on student progress and the improvement of their linguistic skills.

This book aims to marry research-based evidence with collective experience, not only from my own classroom experience but also from the professional expertise of many colleagues whom I have known and worked with personally in my career or encountered online. As a Twitter user and

Expert teaching requires ...

Challenge
So that ...
Students have high expectations of what they can achieve

Explanation
So that ...
Students acquire new knowledge and skills

Modelling
So that ...
Students know how to apply the knowledge and skills

Students engage in deliberate practice

Questioning
So that ...
Students are made to think hard with breadth, depth and accuracy

Feedback
So that ...
Students think about and further develop their knowledge and skills

Scaffolding

follower of the #mfltwitterati hashtag, it is clear that we MFL teachers are a creative, passionate, resilient and generous bunch. I never cease to be amazed by the high-quality engagement and sharing which happens in the MFL edu-Twitter sphere. While no book could ever adequately reference the astonishing array of superb resources and ideas to be found there, I hope that I can provide a flavour of the compelling benefits for student learning and outcomes when strong research aligns with the professional wisdom and expertise of practitioners – leading to effective classroom pedagogy and, in turn, to high-quality learning resources. This book seeks to provide practical strategies that are accessible to all MFL teachers, no matter what stage of their career.

The framework for this will be the six interrelated pedagogical principles shared by Shaun Allison and Andy Tharby in the original *Making Every Lesson Count* book: challenge, explanation, modelling, practice, feedback and questioning.[13]

These principles undoubtedly form the essentials for great teaching, transcending subject-specific boundaries. MFL teaching is no exception. High expectations and strong challenge in the classroom, coupled with effective approaches to modelling, guided and deliberate student practice and robust feedback, can serve to expedite the linguistic progression of our students and enhance outcomes. If we employ high-quality and strategic approaches to our explanations and questioning, we will facilitate the learning process further.

Allison and Tharby make it clear that their approach is what they call 'tight but loose'. We are free to implement and connect the six principles as we see fit. This is particularly pertinent in the case of modern foreign languages, which are unique due to the fact that much of the content is delivered in a different language. This has evident implications

---

13 Shaun Allison and Andy Tharby, *Making Every Lesson Count: Six Principles to Support Great Teaching and Learning* (Carmarthen: Crown House Publishing, 2015).

for the aforementioned filter we deploy when considering, for example, what effective questioning and high-quality explanation looks like in our subject.

Taking this into account, this book aims to explore each principle and its implications for the MFL classroom in detail. Each chapter will include both a discussion of the underpinning theory and practical strategies for how it can be realised. The book is not a silver bullet, and nor should the principles serve as a lesson plan or some sort of pre-scribed hierarchy for use. The strategies suggested for each principle may work for some but not for others. Each school, MFL department, classroom and their respective cultural context is different, and it is up to you to decide which strat-egies you feel may be most useful and applicable. No doubt you will also be able to enrich the strategies by adding your own ideas and thoughts to what is presented.

The underpinning principle is *challenge*. Students rise or fall according to the level of expectation we set for them. As we will see in Chapter 1, challenge is multilayered and permeates everything from MFL curriculum design, the culture and ethos we establish in the classroom and the strategies we employ to ensure that our students meet aspirational learn-ing goals. While at times it may feel like an easy route to lower expectations in order to get some potential quick wins, especially with more reticent and disengaged learners, we should not shy away from embracing struggle in the class-room as we cumulatively expose students to the intricacies of linguistic structure and develop their ability to use language explicitly and confidently in ever more advanced contexts. The success that our students hopefully experience following struggle will, in turn, feed back into motivation and confi-dence in their linguistic development. That success may be something as simple as accurate responses in retrieval prac-tice quizzes, a word of praise from their teacher following a target language sentence which has been well constructed and pronounced, or affirmation of development in written skills, both in terms of fluency and accuracy.

As MFL teachers we present language on a daily basis, whether in terms of individual items of vocabulary, grammatical structures or linguistic form. This initial input on the part of the teacher not only helps to consolidate challenge and expectation, but also sets the scene for follow-up linguistic input in the form of listening and reading activities and establishes the bar of expectation for student output. Chapter 2 on *explanation* will look at strategies that we can employ in order to do this most effectively, with a particular focus on our initial presentation of language, structure and form in the classroom.

In the classroom arena, decluttered from the trappings and distractions of search engines, websites and internet translation tools, the teacher as expert has the scope to lead the (co-)construction and deconstruction of models of excellence with students in the target language. This is why *modelling* is so important as a concept in the MFL classroom. We will explore this further in Chapter 3 and identify some tips and techniques for maximising its potential.

Practice matters a great deal in our classrooms. While we may be able to explain and model very effectively, we risk impeding a student's learning if it is not backed up by robust practice. As Daisy Christodoulou outlines in her book *Making Good Progress?*, practice is absolutely vital for skill development.[14] If we want our students to become highly skilled linguists, we must afford them as many opportunities as possible to practise and master linguistic concepts for the sake of both fluency and accuracy. Chapter 4 will explore the purpose of practice in the MFL classroom, with a nod to current research, before branching off into the specific skills of listening, speaking and reading, and identifying potential strategies for maximising practice in these skills in our classrooms.

---

14 Daisy Christodoulou, *Making Good Progress? The Future of Assessment for Learning* (Oxford: Oxford University Press, 2016), p. 46.

The benefit of giving students good and timely *feedback* has a substantial weight of research evidence behind it. Providing feedback is one of the most effective – and cost-effective – ways of improving students' learning. The strategies in Chapter 5 will focus on three areas: how to improve the quality of in-the-moment feedback, how to improve the efficacy and quality of marking and how to improve approaches to peer and self-checking.

Finally, Chapter 6 will explore approaches to *questioning* which straddle all the other principles. Questioning can give us as MFL teachers a powerful insight into where our students are in their learning and how we need to respond in our teaching approaches. It also considers methods we can employ to enhance greater target language use by students in the classroom.

A current theme in each chapter will be the lessons emerging from cognitive science about learning and memory. This book aims to demonstrate the potential these lessons hold for MFL curriculum design, content and classroom pedagogy, and how they may have a bearing on the decisions we make, not least in relation to which resources and even textbooks we use. In turn, there is the possibility of creating a learning pathway for our students which allows them to build their linguistic knowledge cumulatively and confidently with ever-increasing fluency and accuracy. In this manner they build effectively on prior learning and experience opportunities to transfer deepening knowledge into ever new and expanding contexts. Without this coherent programme, which prioritises the embedding of linguistic forms and structures in long-term memory, we risk our MFL curriculum becoming a disjointed and demotivating experience for our students. Our aim must always be to continually construct and build on their mental schema in long-term memory, as this is when we know that real learning is taking place.

Teachers of MFL, in particular, have a very privileged position. To return to John le Carré's musings on MFL teaching, he states: "It's a promise to educate – yes – and to equip. But also to awaken; to kindle a flame that you hope will never go out; to guide your pupils towards insights, ideas and revelations that they would never have arrived at without your dedication, patience and skill."[15]

Los geht's! On y va! Vamos! Let's get started!

---

15 le Carré, Why We Should Learn German.

Chapter 1

Challenge

It's the first French lesson of Year 7, and Mrs Pentland introduces herself to the twenty-eight eager, enthusiastic 11-year-olds seated before her. Having taught for nineteen years, she recognises that familiar frisson of excitement insider her at the thought of being in a position to instil a love of languages and language learning in these students and of being the person charged with moulding them into competent and proficient linguists.

As she does every year, Mrs Pentland asks the class if any of them know any French. About half the hands in the room shoot up. Harry tells her that they learnt French for two years in primary school, and proudly tells her that he can count to 50. She dutifully commends him on this, but seeing the glint of panic in the eyes of Serena, the little girl beside Harry who did not attend the same school, she does not ask Harry to display his knowledge. Jason speaks up to say that he attended the languages club at his primary school and knows the words for lots of animals. When Mrs Pentland then asks the class who has been to France, again approximately half the hands in the room go up. Molly announces that she goes with her family every year for three weeks to Provence, and speaks with gusto about her morning excursions for delicious pain au chocolat in the village bakery and about watching the daily games of pétanque in the early evenings. Mrs Pentland also knows from experience that some students in the class have probably never travelled abroad before.

Turning to the board to explain the lesson's learning intentions, she has another familiar thought – the same thought she has every year. In the modern languages classroom, teachers are not starting with a blank canvas. Each student is bringing with them into the classroom varying degrees of knowledge, cultural experience and preconceptions. In ensuring that all the students are challenged in their language learning, she herself will be challenged to adopt the most effective teaching approaches and strategies. Mrs Pentland knows that she is well up for the challenge!

The example of Mrs Pentland's Year 7 class, as they transition to secondary school, highlights how it is not always an even playing field in our MFL classrooms. Some students will come with prior exposure to the language at primary school, either through formal curricular time or extracurricular opportunities such as a languages club. While these students often look forward to their secondary school language learning experience and are initially keen to demonstrate their prior knowledge, let's bear in mind all the potential 'Serenas' who have not been exposed to languages at primary level, and who may already be forming a preconception that they are at a disadvantage or behind in their learning. Sometimes during our teaching careers we may also, of course, teach bilingual young people who have grown up in a household where the foreign language is a means of communication, either primarily or partly.

Alongside these varying levels of knowledge, there is the question of the cultural capital which our students have gained before transitioning to secondary school. Some will have visited the target language country, either once or twice or on a repeated basis. They will have gleaned cultural experiences which will, in turn, have fashioned their perceptions of the country's culture and language in a mostly positive manner. They will have formed an array of anecdotes which will act as a point of reference as they study the language further. This melange of prior experience, cultural capital and varying degrees of knowledge can make the provision of challenge for students in the MFL classroom a complex affair. Large class sizes and having to teach MFL within the constraints of a rigid school timetable can add to that complexity.

Challenge as a concept is slightly different from the other five principles in this book. While there are certainly specific teaching strategies that can be employed to ensure that challenge is appropriate for all students at a given time, the concept itself is much more to do with our long-term teaching approaches and therefore should overarch everything. It should run through everything we do – the culture we establish, the teaching strategies we utilise, the routines we embed, the academic register we develop in the classroom (particularly the features of vocabulary and grammar) and the language we use in order to communicate expectations to our students. A little like the fruits, nuts and spices which permeate an exceedingly good German stollen, appropriate challenge gives our lessons their core essence, texture and flavour, and is simply crucial in order to ensure successful outcomes.

Challenge in the modern languages classroom can be defined as the provision of work which causes students to think deeply and engage in healthy 'struggle'. Struggle is healthy when it challenges students in a manner which allows them, over time, to learn effectively. In the specific case of modern foreign languages, appropriately pitched challenge will afford our students opportunities to develop the procedural knowledge of grammar, vocabulary and discourse rules of the language. Ultimately, such challenge will allow them to develop automaticity – being able to draw on long-term memory in order to use and manipulate the language quickly and fluently.

When faced with a difficult class or a class with motivational issues (perhaps on a Friday afternoon!), it may seem like the simpler option to opt for 'quick win' strategies in which students experience some superficial success without struggle. However, this may come at the expense of high challenge and deep thinking, as it often happens within students' comfort zones. An example of this could be spending entire lessons focusing on the acquisition of single-word vocabulary. While this is important as a building block for a student's cumulative linguistic development, our aim should be to provide students with structured opportunities to use vocabulary in context as quickly as possible.

As we will explore further in Chapter 2, vocabulary needs to be owned, used, assimilated and practised deliberately within structures very soon after it is first encountered. The Teaching Schools Council's *Modern Foreign Languages Pedagogy Review* reflects this:

Teachers should know that errorless teaching techniques (when pupils are unambiguously told the meaning of a new word) are effective, providing that rapidly they are required to use the new words in comprehension and then productively. The more times a pupil is required to recall a word, the more securely it will move into the long term memory. Activities or tasks where pupils need to recall or find a particular word in order to complete communication, so filling a genuine information gap, are very helpful in assisting memorisation. Vocabulary should be reinforced by having pupils incorporate it into new sentences they compose themselves.[1]

Putting language into context as soon as possible, strong modelling strategies, effective questioning, high-quality opportunities for students to practise and robust feedback will all help to develop procedural knowledge and automaticity of skill in long-term memory, thus facilitating success and boosting motivation.

The need for our students to experience success in the MFL classroom is crucial. Obtaining a high success rate is one of Barak Rosenshine's ten 'Principles of Instruction' in order to ensure optimal learning outcomes for students.[2] As MFL teachers, however, we should perhaps also bear in mind the very topical issue of retention. We are all aware of the current debate in MFL circles regarding why foreign languages are not attracting greater numbers of candidates at GCSE level. Some of the main reasons given by students for not choosing a language at GCSE are that it is too difficult and they do not have confidence in their language skills. Therefore, the strategies we use in the classroom should offer healthy struggle in a manner which also enables students to experience success.

Our aim as MFL teachers must surely be to keep our students in the healthy struggle zone, where they are thinking hard and where there are plenty of opportunities for deliberate practice which will bring about the kind of genuine success that follows meaningful challenge. This involves using our teaching approaches and strategies to lift them out of their comfort zone, where there may be low stress but ultimately limited challenge and outcomes.

---

1 Bauckham, *Modern Foreign Languages Pedagogy Review*, p. 9.
2 Barak Rosenshine, Principles of Instruction: Research-Based Strategies That All Teachers Should Know, *American Educator* 36(1) (2012): 12–19, 39 at 17. Available at: https://www.aft.org/sites/default/files/periodicals/Rosenshine.pdf.

At the other end of the scale, we must ensure they are not thinking so hard that working memory – where we hold and process information – is overburdened and cognitive overload occurs, leading to limited learning. Our students will be operating primarily from working memory as they sit before us in the classroom. Effective strategies and approaches for keeping students in the struggle zone will involve harnessing that working memory effectively and appropriately. This book will explore such strategies.

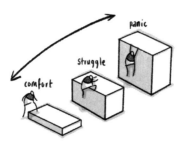

It is important that this culture of high expectation and challenge happens from the outset, in year groups furthest away from high-stakes public examinations. As we have already seen, the students sitting in front of us at the start of their secondary school career may display varying degrees of knowledge, cultural capital and preconceptions. It is our job to synthesise all of this information and then push each student just enough to keep them in the struggle zone.

So, how do we build in high-level challenge for our students? How do we ensure that we as teachers are not being fooled into the false proxy that busy, engaged students equates to high-level challenge? How do we make it normal to do things which are difficult, challenging and academic in our MFL classrooms? Let's explore some strategies.

1. Why First Impressions Count: Keep It 'Unique' and 'Magnifique'

Our students' first exposure to challenge when they enter the classroom may well be in how we formulate learning objectives. The importance of this as an opportunity for anchoring high challenge cannot be overstated. Consider the following learning objectives from a Year 8 lesson:

All students	will be able to recognise ten means of transport in French.
Most students	will be able to spell ten means of transport accurately in French.
Some students	will be able to write sentences to say how they travel to a particular location.

By framing learning objectives in this manner we run the risk – both implicitly and explicitly – of setting the bar low and reinforcing limited challenge.

Firstly, the objectives focus almost entirely on the acquisition of transport vocabulary in French. This paves the way for a very topic-based, vocabulary-driven lesson with the potential for low-challenge activities.

Secondly, the framing of the objectives in this manner has implicitly reinforced a perception that language 'production' (speaking and writing) is somewhat more difficult than language 'reception' (listening and reading). All students are expected to recognise the words whenever they hear them or see them written down, but it is anticipated that only some students will be able to write the means of transport accurately from memory within a short sentence.

Thirdly, as Allison and Tharby point out, framing learning objectives in this manner has the potential to perpetuate low expectations.[3] The less confident or more reticent student may be inclined to settle for the first learning objective for fear of failure or embarrassment if the two more 'challenging' objectives are not met.

Conversely, in anchoring high challenge, it is perhaps much better to opt for one single (unique) and aspirational (magnifique) learning objective, and to ensure that scaffolds are in place to give all students the opportunity to reach those dizzy heights of real achievement.

An alternative learning objective for the Year 8 class may read as follows:

To explore, express and justify in French reasons for using different means of transport.

---

3   Allison and Tharby, *Making Every Lesson Count*, p. 20.

The anchoring of high challenge is perhaps much more evident in this objective:

♦ As opposed to activities focused on single-word vocabulary acquisition, there is the clear implication that students may be exposed to the language in the context of more sophisticated structures and contexts.

♦ The focus on justification draws students' attention to a particular function of language, and aligns with GCSE specifications which refer to this function as a necessity for securing a score in the highest mark scheme band.

♦ As MFL teachers know well, the learning of a foreign language is a functional and cumulative affair. Students build on their prior knowledge of linguistic function – developing, extending and modifying the schema they hold in long-term memory. Students may already have been exposed to the function of giving and justifying opinions within a range of contexts in prior years at a more basic level. Reinforcing the function again at a more advanced level allows students the opportunity to develop and extend their prior knowledge of this linguistic function.

♦ As opposed to a lesson focused on the acquisition of single-word vocabulary, the emphasis on language used in extended sentences and paragraphs allows for a revisit of grammatical structures such as connectives – for example, 'Je n'aime pas voyager en avion parce qu'il faut faire la queue pendant des heures à l'aéroport' (I don't like travelling by plane because you have to queue for hours at the airport).

♦ There is no implicit assumption in the objective regarding the difficulty level of linguistic skill – all students are expected to listen, speak, read and write in the language effectively.

An example of a high-level, high-challenge reading activity to accompany this learning objective for a Year 8 class may look something like this:

LES TRANSPORTS

Je m'appelle Paul. Je vais vous parler des transports en commun.

Je vais au collège en bus. D'habitude je vais en vacances en avion et en car; cependant l'année prochaine nous allons voyager aux Pays-Bas en voiture et en aéroglisseur. Ce sera une expérience insolite!

J'adore voyager en avion parce que c'est rapide et pratique. Par contre, c'est mauvais pour l'environnement et il faut faire la queue pendant des heures à l'aéroport. Je déteste voyager en bateau car j'ai toujours le mal de mer. Quand il fait du vent ou quand il y a des orages, il y a toujours des retards. Je n'aime pas prendre le car parce que je ne peux jamais dormir. C'est assez inconfortable. Je préfère voyager en TGV parce que ce n'est pas cher, et on peut se relaxer en regardant le paysage.

1   Name six means of transport mentioned.

_____ (6)

2   Which country is he travelling to next year?

_____ (1)

3   How is he getting there?

_____ (2)

4   Give two positive and two negative opinions on flying mentioned by Paul.

_____ (2)

_____ (2)

5   What two weather conditions are mentioned?

_____ (2)

6   Give two negative opinions on travelling by
    boat mentioned by Paul.

_____ (2)

7   Give two positive opinions about the last means
    of transport mentioned by Paul.

_____ (2)

TRANSPORT

I am called Paul. I am going to talk to you about public
transport.

I go to school by bus. Normally, I go on holidays by
plane and coach; however, next year we are travelling to
the Netherlands by car and hovercraft. That will be a
one-off experience!

I love travelling by plane because it is quick and practical. On the other hand, it is bad for the environment and
you have to queue for hours at the airport. I hate travelling by boat because I always get seasick. When it is
windy or when there are storms, there are always delays.
I don't like taking the coach because I can never sleep.
It's also quite uncomfortable. I prefer travelling by high-
speed train because it is not expensive, and you can relax
while looking at the landscape.

Not only does this activity orient students' attention to core
transport vocabulary, but it also emphasises linguistic function (opinions and justification) and encourages them to use
their linguistic knowledge and skills (identification of

cognates such as 'faire la queue' and recognition of linguistic heritage in words such as 'dormir' in French and 'dormitory' in English).

Our role as MFL teachers is to support our students to ensure that they reach – or go beyond – aspirational learning objectives. By setting the bar high, we can give all of our students the best opportunities for success.

2. Scale Up

In the previous strategy we unpicked a single, aspirational learning intention about means of transport in French into several components of high challenge. This enabled us to ascertain how proposed challenging activities for the Year 9 class in question might, in fact, meet national assessment criteria at GCSE level at a high level, not least through the function of justifying opinions.

This is a useful rule of thumb when planning for the anchoring of challenge. By taking the expected knowledge base, concepts and skills in our MFL curriculum and teaching just beyond that point, it ensures that our students are being exposed at an early stage to the most challenging concepts of assessment guidelines. This means dipping into GCSE work at Key Stage 3 and A level work during GCSE studies.

It is important here to appreciate the value of strong curriculum planning as a means of anchoring challenge. If we get the level of challenge right in the curriculum, this will drive our teaching.

Experience suggests that students can find it very motivating to be told that they are undertaking work which is above their expected level and which should be intrinsically difficult for them. When we tell our own students this, we should always be careful to build in the rationale by saying something along the lines of, "We are doing this because I as your teacher believe in you, because I believe in your potential to aspire and achieve at a high level. We are going to find it challenging, but if we think logically, lean on our prior knowledge, use our acquired skills and demonstrate resilience, there is a strong chance we will succeed. Your success is very important to me."

As teachers, we perhaps assume that students implicitly appreciate that their success is of great importance to us. However, we should never underestimate the power of articulating it. The explicit articulation of high challenge, expectation and aspiration plays a part in ensuring that our students develop the growth mindset we wish them to have. It is part of that overarching climate of challenge which we should grow in our classrooms.

While the embedding of challenging content into lesson activities in a natural way is a primary goal, I have also been trialling a discrete new initiative with my Year 8 French class called 'Mock Friday'. After break on Fridays, we spend ten minutes undertaking a question from a GCSE reading paper which we then correct together using the visualiser. The question is carefully chosen to tie in with what they are currently studying, of course, and to ensure as far as possible that many of them may experience some success. Students are typically very motivated at the thought of undertaking GCSE-level work three years early, especially when they taste some success in doing so following struggle, and this feeds back into their engagement and motivation in class. This approach also allows for effective retrieval.

In one recent example, my Year 8 class were given a question about a new leisure centre. They were asked to read the French and then complete some sentences in English with words or phrases from the box. The question tested whether students could equate 'sept jours sur sept' (seven days out of seven) from the text with 'every day' from the box as the answer to how many days the centre was open. Students struggled with this. In the ensuing discussion during correction, we retrieved the word 'jour' (day) from the learning of days in Year 7 and talked about how the word 'bonjour' literally means 'good-day'. We also retrieved how the preposition 'sur' meant 'on' or 'on top of' from our description of rooms in a house in Year 7, and how it had been used in this context to indicate frequency of an event. Such opportunities for retrieval, especially after a long period of time and for seeing prior learnt language in new contexts, can be invaluable.

There are also ways in which we can scale up implicitly in our classrooms when teaching topics. For example, a scheme of work on the topic of 'school' may involve students stating preferences on school subjects before going on to describe their school timetable in subsequent weeks, at which point they will be taught how to say clock times in the language. When teaching opinions on school subjects, why not build aspects of time into receptive listening and reading exercises? After all, students will be familiar with numbers and in certain languages may have an understanding of the word for 'half' through previous learning on family members such as 'half-sister'.

3. Space It Out

Those of us familiar with the studies of Robert and Elizabeth Bjork will know about their work on so-called 'desirable difficulties', where they suggest that introducing certain difficulties into the learning process can greatly improve long-term retention of the learnt material because "they trigger encoding and retrieval processes that support learning, comprehension, and remembering".[4] This includes

---

4   Robert Bjork and Elizabeth Bjork, Making Things Hard on Yourself, But in a Good Way: Creating Desirable Difficulties to Enhance Learning. In Morton Gernsbacher, Richard Pew, Leaetta Hough and James Pomerantz (eds), *Psychology and the Real World: Essays Illustrating Fundamental Contributions to Society* (New York: Worth Publishers, 2011), pp. 56–64 at p. 58.

the desirable difficulty of 'spacing' – the concept of returning to acquired material after a period of time.

In the nineteenth century, psychologist Hermann Ebbinghaus undertook some experiments which revealed a trend referred to as the 'forgetting curve'. We quickly forget newly learnt information, even after just a few hours, unless we return to it periodically. It is most effective if we revisit previously acquired information and knowledge after increasingly spaced out periods of time. If students return to their knowledge of a linguistic context regularly over time, they will remember it better. Quite poignant to MFL is the fact that Ebbinghaus used language as the evidence base for his experiment. He taught himself a series of nonsense syllables and then tested himself over time to see how long he could remember them.

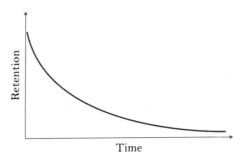

Over time, the retention of the words went down – until the words were reviewed. Then the retention increased. With regular review the 'forgetting time' got longer, so going back over the words made it easier to remember them. The implications are clear: if we want students to be able to remember things, we need to keep returning to them and reviewing them. The benefits of effective spacing in a second language, which is reliant on the cumulative build-up of knowledge and dependent on our students making connections between new content and prior learning, are significant.

A carefully crafted MFL curriculum will ensure that students are revisiting key concepts and structures across topics over months and years as they develop and deepen their schema in long-term memory. MFL teachers might justifiably argue that this happens already and is the core structure of good MFL textbooks. After all, no Spanish teacher would teach the perfect tense once between Year 7 and Year 11 and move on without ever returning to it! Our students must use such an important tense across a range of contexts, and therefore it is natural in our teaching that we revisit it with regularity.

However, do we think about our curriculum design as a five-year plan from Year 7 to Year 11? Do we think explicitly enough about how and when we are spacing the linguistic knowledge over those five years? Do we consider how the desirable difficulty of spacing builds in opportunities to develop and deepen students' linguistic knowledge? Do we consider spacing in terms of linguistic function and not just content, structure and form?

For example, the following table outlines what a student at the end of Year 11 might need to know:

Context	Grammar	Functions
Me, my family and friends	Nouns	Making introductions
Technology in everyday life	Articles	Giving descriptions
Free-time activities	Adjectives	Discussing habits
Customs and festivals in target countries	Adverbs	Expressing and justifying opinions

Context	Grammar	Functions
Home, town, neighbourhood and region	Quantifiers/ intensifiers	Exploring positives and negatives
Social issues	Pronouns	Comparing and contrasting
Global issues	Verbs and tenses	Explaining options
Travel and tourism	Prepositions	Making suggestions
My studies	Conjunctions	Complaining
Life at school	Number, quantity, dates, time	Giving advice
Education post-16		Negotiating arrangements
Jobs, careers, choices and ambitions		Persuading others
		Reporting recent events and expressing future intentions

It is possible to interrogate the MFL curriculum design using a table like this with a focus on spacing. For example:

Context

♦ How might the topic of 'me, my family and friends' be revisited between Years 7 and 11?

  ◊ Year 7: Giving factual statements about family members and pets (how many people in the family, their ages and physical appearance, pets).

  ◊ Year 8: Characteristics of family and friends (personality adjectives).

  ◊ Year 9: Relationships with family members and friends.

  ◊ Year 10: Marriage and partnerships.

Grammar

♦ Where might adjectival rules be taught and reviewed consistently and cumulatively between Years 7 and 11, and how can we ensure they are reviewed across a range of topics?

  ◊ Year 7: Adjectival agreement taught when describing colours of pets.

  ◊ Year 8: Adjectival agreement reviewed and extended when describing personalities of family and friends.

  ◊ Year 8: Comparative and superlative taught when comparing school subjects.

  ◊ Year 9: Comparative and superlative reviewed when talking about relationships with family members and comparing personalities.

Function

♦ What does expressing and justifying opinions look like in Year 7, and how do we build on it as a function in subsequent years to deepen linguistic knowledge, fluency and accuracy?

◊ Year 7: Giving an opinion regarding animals which you like, don't like and prefer, e.g. *J'aime les chats parce qu'ils sont méchants* (I like cats because they are naughty).

◊ Year 7: Giving an opinion and simple justification on school subjects using a connective such as 'because', e.g. *Mathe gefällt mir nicht, weil es schwer ist* (I don't like maths, because it is difficult).

◊ Year 8: Giving an opinion on how you get on with a family member with extended justification, e.g. *Mi hermano es una persona egoísta. Está muy mimado y hace lo que quiere. Nunca me escucha y me insulta todos los días* (My brother is a selfish person. He is very spoiled and does what he wants. He never listens to me and insults me every day).

◊ Year 10: Using the present subjunctive as a connective when giving opinions on marriage, e.g. *J'aimerais bien me marier car je veux faire une grande fête, bien que je me sente obligé(e) d'inviter tout le monde* (I would like to get married because I want to have a big party, even though I feel obliged to invite everybody).

Interrogating the curriculum in this manner allows us to map out a 'big picture' overview of the spaced and cumulative exposure our students will get in relation to contexts/topics, structure/forms and linguistic function over a five-year programme of study. It also allows us to keep challenge at the core of everything we do.

4. Retrieve, Retrieve, Retrieve

Retrieval practice is a strategy which exploits the fact that calling information to mind subsequently enhances and boosts learning. Deliberately recalling information forces us to pull our knowledge 'out' and examine what we know. Through the act of retrieval, or calling information to mind, our memory for that information is strengthened and forgetting is less likely to occur. Retrieval practice makes learning effortful and challenging. Because retrieving information requires mental effort, we often think we are doing poorly if we can't remember something. We may feel that progress is slow, but that is when our best learning takes place. The more difficult the retrieval practice, the better it is for long-term learning.[5]

In their book *Make It Stick: The Science of Successful Learning,* Peter Brown, Henry Roediger and Mark McDaniel discuss the clear links between retrieval and spacing as a desirable difficulty:

To be most effective, retrieval must be repeated again and again, in spaced out sessions so that the recall, rather than becoming a mindless recitation, requires some cognitive effort. Repeated recall appears to help memory consolidate into a cohesive representation in the brain and to strengthen and multiply the neural routes by which the knowledge can later be retrieved.[6]

Retrieval practice refers quite often to the low-stakes quizzing opportunities we build into our lessons and to students' homework. This may be more effective at the start of

---

5   Pooja Agarwal, Henry Roediger, Mark McDaniel and Kathleen McDermott, *How to Use Retrieval Practice to Improve Learning* (St Louis, MO: Washington University, 2013).

6   Peter Brown, Henry Roediger and Mark McDaniel, *Make It Stick: The Science of Successful Learning* (Cambridge, MA: Harvard University Press, 2014), p. 28.

lessons, particularly if we have not seen the class for some days. By the law of averages, many of them will have forgotten some information from the previous lesson. Our students will perform best if they are quizzed at frequent intervals, and if they endeavour to retrieve information from memory instead of just revising it from a book. Thus, spacing can be combined effectively in the form of retrieval practice: low-stakes and regular quizzing of students allows them to retrieve their knowledge of both recently acquired knowledge and knowledge gleaned some time ago.

Most MFL teachers would probably agree that the constraints of school timetabling do not allow for natural cumulative development in language learning. Fitting the learning of a language into two one-hour blocks a week goes against the natural processes needed to learn a language effectively. It is possible that effective retrieval practice in the MFL classroom is a powerful challenge strategy for nullifying the drawbacks of timetabling constraints.

Students struggle with retrieval practice, partly because they are on the cusp of forgetting information and partly because their instinct may well suggest that the best way to revise is through reading notes. Far from it. As we will see in Chapter 4, retrieval practice is a powerful tool for ensuring that every MFL lesson counts.

5. The *Mise en Scène*

Some of the most inspiring MFL classrooms I have visited don't have glossy language posters on the walls which have been bought in a shop or online, they don't have laminated knowledge cards on their walls and they don't even have colourful pictures which have been neatly drawn and labelled in the target language by Year 7 and 8 students. Instead, they have high-level models of excellence in language use, often a paragraph or page which has been written by the students. In one extremely impressive classroom, the teacher had taken time to type out and place underneath each piece of work exactly why it was so brilliant.

If we really want to challenge our students and set the bar of expectation high, we should ensure that from the outset and create a *mise en scène* (the surrounding 'landscape' of the classroom) which allows our students to marvel at the excellence around them. This can take a range of formats, not just wall displays:

♦ An electronic portfolio of excellent work.

♦ Exam scripts from students who have performed at a very high level.

♦ The best exercise books from our most successful students.

♦ Displaying 'live' examples of excellence under the visualiser as our students work in the classroom.

♦ Deconstructing a model of excellence together.

By consistently referring to excellence and brilliance in linguistic use and in the presentation of work, including on parents' evenings and open evenings, we reinforce the high expectations and aspirations we hold for all our students. It is quite possible that students, in turn, will respond to that expectation when they see what has been achieved by their peers and when they realise what is possible in their productive outcomes. It is also true that some students may feel a little intimidated at where and how to start in order to reach such standards. However, with the correct support, including modelling and practice, which we will explore in upcoming chapters, we will hopefully remove any angst our students may feel.

Reflective Questions

♦ How do you embed a culture of high challenge from the very outset of lessons?

♦ How do you ensure that the pitch of the lesson allows for all students to reach aspirational yet accessible learning outcomes and beyond, despite potential differences in prior knowledge?

♦ How do you plan lessons so that they contain challenging learning content which retains students in the struggle zone?

♦ How do you build in opportunities for the emulation and production of excellence in language use, as well as for the development of an academic register?

♦ How do you benchmark brilliant in your classroom in a manner which encourages all students to aspire?

♦ Do you plan frequent opportunities in your lessons for students to retrieve information from memory, thus incorporating the desirable difficulties of spacing and low-stakes testing?

Chapter 2
Explanation

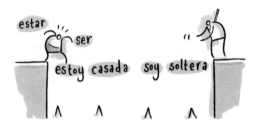

Jenna's Year 10 Spanish class are learning the many different uses of 'ser' and 'estar'. While Jenna has seen and used many sentences with 'ser' and 'estar' in Years 7, 8 and 9, and while she was aware that both verbs meant 'to be', her previous teacher had never explicitly explained why one was being used over the other in these sentences. Jenna had wrongly assumed that it was really quite random whether you selected 'ser' or 'estar'. Now she is beginning to realise the complexities of selecting which verb to use in which circumstances. Her teacher has presented many explanations, including state versus essence, the use of something called the present continuous tense (which Jenna had never heard of before) and even the simple passive formation (which went well over her head). And after all the explanations, Jenna still cannot understand why you use 'estar' to say 'I am married' (*estoy casada*) but use 'ser' to say 'I am single' (*soy soltera*). Jenna concludes that this aspect of Spanish grammar is just far too complicated and she is never going to grasp it.

This example raises a number of interesting issues. The biggest, perhaps, is that Jenna has not been exposed to an explicit and specific explanation of the distinctions between 'ser' and 'estar' in her previous language learning. For a reasonably complex grammatical item with many nuances, it may have helped if her teacher had adopted a step-by-step approach, starting with an initial explicit rule-of-thumb explanation very early on in Jenna's Spanish learning experience appropriate to her level of learning. For example, this might be an explanation which encourages the student to think of 'estar' as referring to 'where' and 'how', and 'ser' to 'who', 'what' and 'when'. This could then be returned to at numerous junctures as she continues her Spanish learning journey, and layered, expanded, analysed and modified as appropriate, adding state, essence and tense usage into the mix. Such an approach, spaced cumulatively over a student's language learning journey, may have helped to avoid the obvious overload Jenna feels in her Year 10 class.

As Andy Tharby outlines, explanation is an art form, albeit a slightly mysterious one. We know when we hear and see a teacher unravelling a great one: "It has something to do with their effortless subject knowledge, the simplicity and directness with which they do it and the sense of assurance they exude. Nevertheless, we struggle to describe the intricacies of the craft."[1]

That struggle to describe exactly why an explanation is good can be equally matched by an MFL teacher's dilemma in deciding how to explain something. Should it be done in the target language or in the student's first language? If done in the target language, how do we ensure that all students have understood? Do we teach the grammar rule explicitly, or do we get the students to infer by working the rule out for themselves?

This makes the art of explanation in the MFL classroom a very different beast from other subjects. Having said that, there are some general principles which we should perhaps consider when planning our explanations:

---

1 Andy Tharby, *How to Explain Absolutely Anything to Absolutely Anyone: The Art and Science of Teacher Explanation* (Carmarthen: Crown House Publishing, 2018), p. 5.

- How do we tether new knowledge to what the students already know? We are more likely to absorb new knowledge if it links to existing schemata in our long-term memories. For example, if students already have a strong understanding of conjugated forms of 'avoir' and 'être', and if they have good knowledge of the need for adjectival agreement after the verb 'être', they are more likely to understand and grasp their use as auxiliary verbs in the perfect tense and the need for agreement for verbs which use 'être' as their auxiliary.

- How can we introduce new ideas in clear steps? We know that there is a limit to what can be held in working memory – this is known as cognitive load.[2] If we try to present too much information to students at once – as is potentially the case with Jenna – we risk overloading working memory, which leads to confusion, frustration and an ultimate lack of real learning.

- How do we avoid the curse of the expert? In the MFL classroom, this may include using target language in our explanations which is beyond some students' reach or using an academic register which is unfamiliar to them. We must be incredibly careful in our explanations not to ignore knowledge that we have and take for granted and that our students do not.

This chapter will explore several strategies for explanation, looking at some ideas for introducing vocabulary and grammar, the premise of chunking, the value of emphasising phonics and the role of anecdotes, songs and mnemonics, among other things.

---

2   Centre for Education Statistics and Evaluation, *Cognitive Load Theory: Research That Teachers Really Need to Understand* (Sydney: NSW Department of Education, 2017). Available at: https://www.cese.nsw.gov.au//images/stories/PDF/cognitive-load-theory-VR_AA3.pdf.

1. Know Thy Lesson

In his article in *researchED*, Steve Smith discusses the tensions which exist in second-language learning research, particularly in relation to the *implicit* acquisition of a second language as opposed to the *explicit* teaching of concepts.[3]

Many researchers into second-language acquisition hold the view that most learning occurs implicitly or subconsciously, just as when young children acquire their first language. We have a biologically primary mental module as human beings which predisposes us to learn how to speak our native language as young children without explicit teaching. Researchers claim that this predisposition may also exist in second-language acquisition. Language learning is somehow 'natural' and therefore different from other forms of learning. Proponents of this research, such as Stephen Krashen, claim that the MFL classroom should primarily aim to reflect the processes of first-language acquisition by trying to provide as much comprehensible language input as possible and opportunities to interact with it.[4]

However, other research purports that language skill is better developed in a similar vein to how other skills are developed – through explicit instruction, modelling, plenty of practice and effective feedback. In light of this tension, Smith – in the aforementioned *researchED* article – argues that MFL teachers should 'hedge their bets' by ensuring that they do two things in lessons: "(1) Exploit natural acquisition mechanisms by using as much of the target language as possible in meaningful and interesting ways, involving listening, speaking, reading and writing; and (2) Exploit the gradual acquisition of skills by using a certain amount of

3 Steve Smith, Single, Bilingual: What Do We Need to Know About Second-Language Learning?, *researchED* (June 2019). Available at: https://researched.org.uk/single-bilingual-what-do-we-need-to-know-about-second-language-learning.

4 Stephen Krashen, *Principles and Practice in Second Language Acquisition* (Oxford: Pergamon Press, 1982). Available at: http://www.sdkrashen.com/content/books/principles_and_practice.pdf.

explanation and structured practice on high-frequency areas of vocabulary and grammar."

One of the best examples I have come across of someone who endeavours to marry these two principles in a manner which maximises classroom time is Dr Gianfranco Conti.[5] For every year group, he selects a set of core items which he calls 'universals' – that is, chunks, patterns and morphemes – which he sets out to teach in every lesson through implicit lesson routines, exposure to texts, production tasks which elicit their deployment and homework. For Year 7, universals include question structures, modal verbs with the infinitive, negative structures and agreement.

Implicit routines which are built into lessons include:

♦ Question time, whereby students construct questions based on a random question structure from a question wheel.

♦ 'Grumpy' time, whereby students must speak and write negative structures.

♦ Register routines, whereby students answer a question in sentences when their name is called.

♦ Small-talk routines, whereby the teacher asks a student a question when other students may be otherwise engaged.

♦ Exit-ticket routines, whereby students answer a question pertinent to the lesson in hand.

Each of these universals is often accompanied by a sentence-builder scaffold, such as the one on pages 46–47, which 'chunks' language for the students in a manner which helps to facilitate the process of embedding it in long-term memory. We will discuss chunking later in this chapter, and in Chapter 4 we will explore how knowledge organisers may be used to chunk language implicitly.

---

5   Gianfranco Conti, Tempus Fugit: Four Strategies to Maximise MFL Curriculum Time, *The Language Gym* [blog] (29 July 2017). Available at: https://gianfrancoconti.wordpress.com/2017/07/29/tempus-fugit-irreparabile-four-strategies-to-maximise-your-curriculum-time. For more information on Conti's approach visit: https://gianfrancoconti.wordpress.com.

¿Por dónde se va al/a la ...? (How do you get to the ...?)

Para ir (to go)	tome (take)		
al mercado (to the market) al polideportivo (to the sports centre) al ayuntamiento (to the town hall) al centro comercial (to the shopping centre) al parque (to the park) al teatro (to the theatre) al restaurante (to the restaurant) al castillo (to the castle) al hospital (to the hospital) al estadio (to the stadium)		la primera calle (the first road) la segunda calle (the second road) la tercera calle (the third road) la cuarta calle (the fourth road)	a la izquierda (on the left) a la derecha (on the right)

Sentence–builder table

	Additional useful phrases to include:		
a la oficina de turismo (to the tourist office) *a la discoteca* (to the disco/nightclub) *a la peluquería* (to the hairdresser) *a la comisaría* (to the police station) *a la iglesia* (to the church) *a la tienda de música* (to the music shop)	*enfrente* (opposite) *detrás* (behind) *delante de* (in front of)	*doble la esquina* (turn the corner) *siga todo recto* (go straight on) *cruce el puente* (cross the bridge) *pase los semáforos* (go through the lights)	*al final de la calle* (at the end of the road) *en el cruce* (at the crossroads) *en los semáforos* (at the traffic lights)

As we can see from the table on pages 50–51, implicit knowledge is accompanied in lessons by explicit exposure to core grammatical items, vocabulary and phonemes. We will explore this in more detail in the rest of this chapter.

2. Core Vocabulary Teaching

As discussed in Chapter 1, it is important that students see vocabulary in context as rapidly as possible. Vocabulary teaching should ensure that students are quickly required to use the word in comprehension and then productively. This not only provides challenge but also ensures that opportunities for recall are enhanced. Lessons that are focused solely on the learning of single-word and topic-related vocabulary, often out of context, do little to build in challenge and ultimately to inspire our students. Activities which oblige them to retrieve the vocabulary for the purposes of filling an information gap in communication heighten the potential for strong memorisation.

In addition, modern languages courses which are built around themes such as 'house and home' and 'the environment' mean that teachers are often using topic-related, specialist vocabulary as the vehicle for vocabulary teaching. A potential issue with this is that the vocabulary we teach may be used relatively rarely and therefore it is hard to build in opportunities to return to it later. Year 7 students, for example, may learn the word for 'cow' when looking at the topic of pets and animals. While there is no problem with this, it is possible that they will never return to this word in the remainder of the Key Stage 3 curriculum. The next time they might use it may be at Key Stage 4 in their own productive outputs for speaking or writing exams – for example, if they live on a farm and are describing it. At this point, they may have forgotten the word altogether.

In order to embed challenge and guarantee we are giving students every chance to master basic concepts in the language early on, we should therefore ensure that we are also building in high-frequency verbs to our lessons from an early stage, as well as plenty of opportunities to return to them.

Our students should also understand the notions of infinitive and stem early on, as this is the foundation they will need in order to manipulate these verbs effectively at a later stage. This is an important aspect of our lexical explanations which is often overlooked. How often do we analyse our MFL curriculum to ensure that the presentation of high-frequency verbs is embedded at an early stage? How do we ensure that our MFL course structure allows for constant revisiting of high-frequency verbs? For example:

to be	to have	to go	to do
to be able to	to say	to want to	to know
to see	to have to	to come	to follow
to speak	to take	to look at	to believe
to think	to wait for	to find	to let
to give	to like	to need	

Implicit route	Explicit route
1 **Universals:** Chunks, patterns and lexical items which cut across all units of work and must be recycled as much as possible throughout each unit, possibly in every lesson. • Question structures (e.g. *Qu'est-ce que, commest est-il …?*) • Phrases + infinitives (e.g. *Je peux, Je veux, Je dois, Je vais, J'ai envie de, J'en ai marre de*) • Negative structures (e.g. *ne … pas, ne … jamais, ne … rien*) • Phrases used to compare and contrast (e.g. *plus … que …*) • Phrases used to express and support opinions (e.g. *Je pense que, Je crois que*) • Phrases used to describe events, places, people (e.g. *c'est, il paraît, il a l'air*) • Phrases used to express emotions and physical states (e.g. *Je me sens triste, Je suis fatigué(e)*)	1 **Core grammar structures:** Grammar structures you want your students to have routinised by the end of the year. 2 **Core vocabulary:** Lexical items you want your students to have routinised by the end of the year. This will include high frequency multi-word chunks and single words. 3 **Core phonemes:** Phonological patterns you want your students to have routinised by the end of the year.

- Time markers (e.g. *tous les jours, le soir, de temps en temps*)

- Connectives and other discourse markers (e.g. *tout d'abord, en fin de compte, vu que*)

- Expressions indicating locations (e.g. *près de, loin de*)

2 **'Seed-planting' items:** These are items that you are planning to teach explicitly in the next unit and to expose the students to already in the current unit to pave the ground for future learning. For instance, at the end of Year 7 (term 3) in the unit on daily routine you will teach a number of reflexive verbs in the first person of the present.

Source: Gianfranco Conti, Tempus Fugit: Four Strategies to Maximise MFL Curriculum Time, *The Language Gym* [blog] (29 July 2017). Available at: https://gianfrancoconti.wordpress.com/2017/07/29/tempus-fugit-irreparabile-four-strategies-to-maximise-your-curriculum-time.

It is also useful when presenting vocabulary to take the time to explore similar roots in the first language as well as potential patterns. This comparison with the first language helps to reinforce patterns, embed the word in the memory and ultimately improve students' metalinguistic skills. This may include:

♦ An exploration of German verb prefixes such as 'ent-', 'emp-' and 'ver-', and the implications we can infer for their meaning.

♦ Making explicit reference to cognates and words with shared roots, such as 'Fenster' (German), 'fenêtre' (French) and 'fenestra' (English).

Of course, we will also have to make our students aware that patterns are not always consistent and that 'false friends' exist in all languages!

At GCSE level, we would want our students to be able to use synonyms and antonyms in their responses. Examples in French might include:

♦ *d'habitude – normalement*

♦ *puis – ensuite*

♦ *de temps en temps – parfois – quelquefois*

There is also a growing body of thought that the study of etymology and linguistics needs to have a greater explicit presence within the MFL curriculum. The Teaching Schools Council's *Modern Foreign Languages Pedagogy Review* states:

> *We recommend that standard grammatical terminology is taught to pupils. This has sometimes been eschewed by teachers in recent decades, but we see no reason to do so. Giving pupils clear knowledge of accepted terminology is empowering and facilitates application of concepts associated with that terminology in different contexts, including in future language learning.*[6]

6   Bauckham, *Modern Foreign Languages Pedagogy Review*, p. 10.

If we want our students to master a second language with ultimate fluency, it is important that we give them the academic register in order to describe their linguistic use cogently and accurately. For a Year 7 French class, this may involve learning the terms grave, acute, circumflex, cedilla and trema and learning about their respective origins and the meaning of their usage. It may also involve, for example, learning about liaison and its implications for pronunciation.

While such etymological understanding may not be explicitly assessed in public exams, there is no doubt that having such background knowledge can only serve to enhance and enrich the language learning experience, deepen metalinguistic understanding and assist the students on their journey from novice to expert.

3. Emphasise the Phonics

The *Modern Foreign Languages Pedagogy Review* makes clear that there is significant evidence, including from the most experienced practitioners, to indicate that direct and systematic teaching of phonics in the very early stages of a student's language learning journey is a reliable method for assuring accurate pronunciation and spelling. If we do not plan to explicitly teach the phonics of the language, it is likely that our students may end up making more errors in communication. However, this is probably still not common practice in a lot of MFL classrooms. Nor, until recently, did I focus on it. However, teaching Year 7 students the accurate pronunciation of sounds such as '-oi', '-eu', '-ai', -'ou' and '-ie' by using phonically challenging words (e.g. *Monsieur*) and then drawing links with other words with the same vowel combinations, can be a very useful strategy in laying the foundations for a lot of what follows, not least reading out loud.

4. Use of Songs

I am utterly convinced that songs are a powerful memorisation tool in the teaching of language structures. And it's fun. Younger students love it, and even if Year 8s and 9s may give a bit of a pantomime grunt at the thought of having to sing, deep down I think that most of them secretly love it too!

Last year, I taught my Year 7 class the weather in French. As part of that process, we learnt a song to the tune of the football chant 'Here We Go':

Il fait beau, il fait chaud, il fait froid,

Il fait du vent, il fait du soleil, il fait du brouillard,

Il pleut, il neige, et il gèle,

Il fait du soleil, il fait beau!

Note that it was structured to ensure that the three phrases without 'fait' were put together on the same line. As a class we rehearsed it, had competitions to see which row sang it best, had fun singing 'brouillard' in funny voices and raised the roof with the final word. The repeated singing, and our enjoyment thereof, had one notable effect: it stuck in the memory. I was absolutely gobsmacked more than a year later when – having come across a weather phrase in a reading activity – the entire class spontaneously broke into song, and it was word perfect too!

Some textbooks come with really good songs, and YouTube is a great resource for finding songs, raps and even beats which can be used to enhance vocabulary presentation. Quite often, the instrumental backgrounds mean that – should you come into my own class when we are singing a song – you may find the students doing a bit of air guitar or air drumming as well!

Songs can be used to introduce key language relevant to the curriculum, to assist with the chunking of linguistic structures in long-term memory (see the next strategy) or for the purposes of comprehension practice.

Gianfranco Conti suggests that, in order to have real learning impact, songs in the target language must have a number of common features, including strong linguistic relevance to curricular aims and 'memorability'.[7] Memorability includes high-frequency linguistic content, repetitive and patterned lyrics, a catchy tune, a song which tells a story where possible and linguistic devices such as alliteration and rhyme.

As a teacher of German, I often use a song with A level students by a group called Tic Tac Toe entitled 'Warum?' (Why?), which deals with the sad death of one of their friends due to drug abuse (thus linking to social issues). It is a catchy tune, and pertinently contains some advanced and rich vocabulary and structures relevant to the topic. A typical lesson sequence incorporating the song would run as follows:

1   Triggering prior knowledge: Some warm-up listening, speaking and reading activities designed to allow the students to retrieve relevant vocabulary and structures already acquired, potentially at GCSE level (e.g. smoking, alcohol, peer pressure, addiction).

---

7   Gianfranco Conti, How to Exploit the Full Learning Potential of an L2 Song in the Classroom, *The Language Gym* [blog] (15 June 2015). Available at: https://gianfrancoconti.wordpress.com/2015/06/15/how-to-exploit-the-full-learning-potential-of-a-target-language-song-in-the-mfl-classroom.

2   An initial listen followed by key questions in the target language:

- How many singers are there?

- Do they sound happy? Sad? Angry? Anxious?

- What words do you recognise?

- What do you think the song might be about?

3   Targeted listening: a cloze exercise whereby the students must complete a transcript by filling in missing words which they hear in the song.

4   Comprehension: The students must match particular phrases in English with relevant lyrics from the text. In 'Warum' these include:

- *Uns gehörte die Welt* (we owned the world).

- *Ich konnte immer auf dich bauen* (I could always rely on you).

- *Ich ahnte die Gefahr* (I sensed the danger).

- *Ich wollte nicht verstehen* (I didn't want to understand).

- *Nur für den Kick, für den Augenblick?* (just for a kick, for this moment?).

- *Für ein Stück von dem falschen Glück* (for a piece of false happiness).

5   Modified output in which structures and phrases gleaned from the song are used to discuss and debate aspects of the topic:

- *Man ahnt selten die Gefahr, wenn man harte Drogen nimmt* (People rarely sense the danger when they take hard drugs).

- *Man nimmt Drogen, um seine Probleme zu vergessen, aber es ist oft ein Stück von dem falschen Glück* (People take drugs to forget their problems, but it is often a piece of false happiness).

Another great song I use with my GCSE German students is 'Millionär' by Die Prinzen, which focuses on the theme of money. Gianfranco Conti and Steve Smith have written at length about the effective use of songs in the MFL classroom in their book *Breaking the Sound Barrier: Teaching Language Learners How to Listen.*[8]

5. Chunking

One of the reasons I believe that songs and raps work so well is because they often 'chunk' lexical items so effectively. In other words, they provide students with ready-to-use language phrases which can be used and modified productively to communicate. Such chunks, learnt implicitly, can be unpacked and analysed at a later stage more explicitly, particularly for grammatical understanding.

Chunking is a strategy which aims to make more efficient use of working memory by breaking information into manageable chunks. These chunks are more easily committed to long-term memory and reduce cognitive load.

As we have already discussed, one of our aims when presenting new language should be to enable students to see vocabulary in context as quickly as possible. In doing so, we are also facilitating opportunities to teach useful linguistic phrases in chunks. Chunking may be presented in the classroom through targeted reading activities, sentence-builder templates which act as a foundation for speaking and writing, songs and even knowledge organisers.

In my own school, when we roll out knowledge organisers we are careful to think about what lexical chunks we want our

---

8   Gianfranco Conti and Steve Smith, *Breaking the Sound Barrier: Teaching Language Learners How to Listen* [Kindle edn] (Authors, 2019), loc. 4118.

students to have acquired over time, primarily through our PROFS (past, reasons, opinions, future, subjunctive) sequence. We want our students to possess these chunks in their long-term memories for a number of reasons. We will explore knowledge organisers and PROFS further in Chapter 4.

Firstly, when these lexical chunks become automatic in memory they free up working memory in the classroom. Secondly, it facilitates the students' ability to manipulate and modify language effectively, using the chunks as a spring-board. Thirdly, the students are implicitly aware of patterns which will assist deep learning when structures are eventually taught explicitly.

Examples of PROFS chunks that my Year 7 Spanish students might know implicitly by the end of the year are included in the table on pages 60–61.

The grouping of lexical chunks in this manner should give students opportunities to identify patterns more easily and manipulate language more readily.

6. Use of Mnemonics and Stories

Telling a story or anecdote in an MFL classroom can be a more nuanced affair than in other subjects. We may tell a story in the students' first language on occasions in order to explain certain cultural points – a story perhaps from our own time of living and working in a target language country. Recounting a story in the target language is a much harder prospect. However, there are many creative ways we can use anecdotes and stories to help our students remember particular lexical or grammatical items. In her blog, Jess Lund, head of sixth form at the Michaela School in Wembley, remembers an example from Barry Smith's classroom when he was teaching days of the week:

Lundi. *Rhymes with Monday. It's the day we go to the moon – the French for 'moon' is 'lune', so it's 'moon day' in both English and French.*

Mardi. *On Tuesdays we go to Mars. Every day in French except Sunday ends in '-di'. It's really easy to remember. Tuesday we go to Mars, so it's mardi.*

Mercredi. *On Wednesdays, we go to Mercury, and we get there in a red Merc. merc-red-i. 8 letters.*

Jeudi. *On Thursdays, we go to Jupiter. When we're there, we play 'un jeu', which is 'a game' in French. ...*

Vendredi. *On Fridays, we go to Venus. When we get there, we find a vending machine, and guess what? It's red. vend-red-i. ...*

Samedi. *Saturdays are so boring – everything is the SAME. I do the same thing every samedi.*

Dimanche. *I have a word of warning for you. You will DIe if you go to MANCHEster with a MAN who eats CHEese on a Sunday. Don't ever do it.*[9]

The use of mnemonics also has its place. Most French teachers will be aware of MRS VAN DER TRAMP, MRS D. VAN DER TRAMP or DR VAN DER TRAMP as aides-memoire for verbs which use 'être' as their auxiliary in the perfect tense.

Mnemonics often relate to exam techniques – for example:

♦ PALM: people, action, location, mood (GCSE photo cards)

♦ DOTTY: description, opinion, tense, tense, yet another opinion (GCSE photo cards)

♦ PEEL: point, evidence, explain, link back to question (A level essays)

---

9   Jess Lund, Aides-mémoire – 1. CUDDLES, *JLMFL* [blog] (15 January 2017). Available at: https://jlmfl.wordpress.com/2017/01/15/aides-memoire-1-cuddles.

P	R	O	F	S
he comido (I have eaten)	*porque me molesta* (because it bothers me)	*en mi opinión* (in my opinion)	*voy a ir* (I am going to go)	*es importante que estudies* (it's important that you study)
he jugado (I have played)	*porque ellos son* (because they are)	*pienso que* (I think that)	*voy a tomar* (I am going to take)	*es bueno que tengas* (it's good that you have)
he observado (I have observed)	*porque me asustan* (because they scare me)	*creo que* (I believe that)	*voy a tener* (I am going to have)	*quizás lo puedan hacer* (maybe they can do it)
he trabajado (I have worked)	*porque es divertido* (because it is enjoyable)	*me gusta* (I like)	*voy a dar* (I am going to give)	*cuando estés conmigo iremos por un helado* (when you're with me we'll go for ice cream)

hemos viajado (we have travelled)		no me gusta (I don't like)	vamos a hablar (we are going to speak)	no creo que vaya a llover (I don't think it's going to rain)
hemos comprado (we have bought)		me gustaría mucho (I would like very much)	vamos a salir (we are going to go out)	aunque esté muy cansada (even if I'm very tired)
he hecho (I have done)		lo que más me gusta es (what I like the most is)	vamos a ver (we are going to see)	

Examples of PROFS chunks

♦ CROATIANS: connectives, reasons, opinions, adjectives, tenses/time phrases, intensifiers, adverbs, negatives, subjunctive (writing)

Mnemonics and stories can act as aides-memoire for our students, whether in the recollection of vocabulary, syntax, sentence structures or even in the development of exam techniques for extended writing.

7. Grammar Teaching

In the 1990s and 2000s, explicit and formal grammar explanation in the MFL classroom was eschewed in some quarters. This was partly due to a (misguided) belief that a communicative approach to language teaching necessitated grammatical inference as opposed to explicit teaching. As a consequence, I have witnessed students with limited explicit exposure to grammar experience success at GCSE level because the assessments were geared towards a communicative approach, only to flounder at A level because their knowledge of basic core grammatical concepts was lacking.

Grammar is clearly indispensable if we are to become fluent in a language. As a result, our curriculum design for MFL must ensure that grammar instruction is well-planned and cumulative from the outset. Without it, we risk demotivating our students and failing to prepare them for language study at a more advanced level.

Textbooks can be somewhat hit and miss when it comes to the cumulative build-up of grammatical knowledge. As yet, I have not come across one textbook that can sit alone in this regard without being supplemented by our own school booklets, worksheets and student notes.

There are potentially four approaches which should be combined in order to ensure effective grammatical explanation in our classrooms:

1   **Teach it explicitly.** Teach the grammar rule from the outset. Outline the form, meaning and use. Make comparisons and connections with the students' first language. Use the academic register of the grammatical rule.

2   **Practise the rule through comprehensible input.** Provide listening and reading tasks which require students to identify the grammatical aspect, normally with other contextual clues stripped away. As the *Modern Foreign Languages Pedagogy Review* outlines, this aspect of grammar practice is underdeveloped in many contexts and not well supported by many course books.[10] Too often, teaching jumps from a formal explanation straight to a demand to use the grammar productively. This can lead to poor mastery.

3   **Scaffold opportunities for students to use the grammatical feature productively.** In order to harness working memory, offer students scaffolds such as a sentence-builder template including parts of structures and sentences, thereby requiring them to focus solely on the grammatical form being taught.

4   **Produce the grammatical form in free writing and speech.** The structured practice afforded in points 2 and 3 above should enable students to use the grammatical form in free speech and written work.

---

10 Bauckham, *Modern Foreign Languages Pedagogy Review*, pp. 10–11.

8. Find the Sweet Spot

As already mentioned, we should try to tether new knowledge to existing knowledge or schemata. In order to do this, we must ascertain what the students already know or can remember. Additionally, we must find out what misconceptions they may have so that we can address them and facilitate their understanding. We need to locate the 'sweet spot' – that is, what they know that is helpful, what they know that is not helpful and how we can build on it. This often helps us to pitch our explanations and presentation of language at the right level.

There are a number of ways we can do this.

♦ **Tell me what you know about …** Before starting a new context at GCSE level, for example, it may be worthwhile to question students on their prior knowledge under a number of subheadings. This may take the form of a template page with columns on it which students complete in the target language in a think-pair-share activity.

Let's take the topic of 'food and eating out' as an example (see table on page 65).

The focus on verbs allows us to ensure that potential high-frequency verbs stay high up on our agenda and are not overshadowed by very specific food-related vocabulary. High-frequency verbs in this topic may include 'to take', 'to have', 'to be' and 'to go', as well as more specific food-related verbs such as 'to cook' and 'to order'.

♦ **Visual prompt:** For more advanced learners, introduce a topic by showing the students an image that links to the topic and then questioning them on it. In the first year of A level study, you may wish to link back to GCSE photo cards (if the exam specification you used involved assessment by photo card). For example, the introduction of a topic on social media in Year 12 may involve showing

Food	Drink	Other vocabulary	Justification	Common verbs	Chunked structures
chicken	milk	bill	salty	to eat	I have eaten
potatoes	water	money	delicious	to drink	We will drink
ham	juice	change	tasty	to take	I will take
beans	wine	menu	sweet	to order	although it was salty
cake	coffee	fork	spicy	to have	I would go to the ice-cream parlour
pasta	tea	spoon	sour	to taste	We ordered
yoghurt	beer	oven	bitter	to go	I have to complain
sea food	lemonade	microwave	disgusting	to complain	near the window

students a photo of young people totally immersed in their phones with questions such as:

◊ What do you see in this image?

◊ What do you think they are doing on their phones?

◊ How many hours a day do you think they spend on social media?

◊ What are the advantages of its use?

◊ What are the disadvantages?

Reflective Questions

♦ How do you keep your own knowledge of the target language up to date?

♦ How do you tether new knowledge to what students already know?

♦ How do you ensure that high-frequency words permeate throughout your teaching?

♦ How do you provide explanations in the target language (if applicable) in a way that is accessible to all students?

♦ How do you chunk up language in order to facilitate the acquisition of patterns and rules and enhance communication skills?

Chapter 3

Modelling

Mr Metcalfe took on a Year 10 French class in September. Now it is April, and he believes it is time for his class to attempt their first GCSE-style written task. He has waited until a range of vocabulary, structures and grammar have been taught cumulatively and in context – for example, the perfect tense within the topic of 'free-time activities', the future tense within the topic of 'travel and tourism' and the conditional tense within the topic of 'jobs and career choices'. Mr Metcalfe sets the class the task of writing approximately 150 words for homework in response to two bullet points in French:

♦ *Décris les aspects positifs de ton école* (Describe the positive things about your school).

♦ *Décris un évènement récent dans ton école* (Describe a recent event in your school).

Mr Metcalfe shares the mark scheme with his students, outlining the marks available for content, range of language and accuracy, and advises them that they may use their notes to assist them.

When the tasks are taken in for marking, Mr Metcalfe feels disappointed. Some students have focused extensively on school subjects; Sally, for example, has written about her personal dislike for certain subjects, even though the task asked her to define the positive aspects of her school.

Accuracy is also a concern for Mr Metcalfe, with many major and minor errors in verb conjugations and tense usage. While opinions were often justified, Mr Metcalfe notes inaccuracies in the use of subordinate clauses.

And then there is Ben, who has quite clearly used an internet translator in an attempt to construct very complex structures – with disastrous results!

No doubt many MFL teachers will relate to and empathise with aspects of Mr Metcalfe's dilemma. I remember a few years ago asking my own Year 10 class to do a similar task in which they outlined in French the free-time activities they enjoyed and a recent activity they had undertaken. When one of my students wrote about going to see 'une allumette [matchstick] de Liverpool FC', the 'dodgy internet translation' warning bells started to sound.

Why is Modelling Important in the Language Classroom?

To be fair, there is much rich and authentic language available online; however, students in our classrooms, like Ben, are potentially nowhere near expert enough in their language learning to be able to discern independently any accurate and high-level language they may locate from the often rather dubious offerings of internet translation services. This is just one of the reasons why modelling in MFL lessons is so important. In the classroom arena, decluttered from the trappings and distractions of search engines and websites, the teacher as expert has the scope to lead the (co-) construction and deconstruction of models of excellence with students.

Mr Metcalfe's task throws up other issues which may be familiar to MFL teachers. Some students have interpreted the task narrowly, choosing to focus extensively on an aspect of school life which is deeply personal to themselves – notably subjects and their opinions thereof. In Sally's case, she even interpreted the task wrongly, focusing on negative opinions when what had been specifically requested was a positive outlook on school. Such a narrow and misaligned response will impact on marks awarded for content and range of language. Had Mr Metcalfe explicitly modelled a task response prior to the students completing it, they may have understood more clearly the need for variety, depth and richness of language. A few sentences to describe school facilities, for example, would have allowed for broadened vocabulary usage and greater adjectival opportunities.

There is also the issue of how well students can transfer grammatical knowledge and consequent accuracy into slightly different contexts. If the perfect tense has been taught within the topic of 'free-time activities', and students were exposed to examples of perfect tense use within that contextual framework, how effectively will they transfer their knowledge of the perfect tense to describe a memorable school event? Some students may be able to manipulate their knowledge appropriately, but others may not.

Additionally, just because something has been taught does not necessarily mean that it has been learnt. This can be very evident in a subject like MFL, which demands outcomes based on the cumulative build-up of knowledge. I remember some years ago teaching my GCSE German class the future tense within the context of 'holidays', and backing it up with numerous explicit worksheets which aimed to demonstrate the future tense in various styles and registers, including a range of personal pronouns. After a few weeks of intense classroom focus on the topic, the students performed well in a test on the future tense given immediately afterwards. Yet four months later, their Year 10 internal exam responses demonstrated some significant inaccuracies.

It is hard not to experience a slight sinking feeling whenever this happens. Quite often we might find ourselves saying, "But I taught them that!" I'm sure this is an experience that many MFL teachers can empathise with, whether it is the intricate distinctions between 'ser' and 'estar' in Spanish, German prepositions with the dative case or French verb conjugations. The reality is that students may have 'performed' at the time it was taught based on the short-term knowledge in their working memory, but it has not embedded in long-term memory. Performing well immediately after a period of classroom teaching focused narrowly on one aspect of linguistic production, such as a specific tense, is very different from the demonstration of learning some months down the line in an exam paper which asks students to produce an outcome with breadth and depth of content, linguistic range and accuracy.

The importance of modelling excellent writing in the MFL classroom cannot be underestimated. It enables teachers to build in strategies which aim to embed linguistic awareness and understanding in long-term memory. Modelling is a process which is led by the teacher as expert and assisted by the students as novices. Robust modelling can allow teacher and students to benchmark excellence through that process, to identify and discuss where mistakes and misconceptions may be likely to occur, and to draft, edit and refine responses based on a strong understanding of mark schemes. Modelling which incorporates the principles of spacing and interleaving will give students the chance to develop their skill in manipulating language through the transfer of concepts into a range of topic areas. Co-construction of a model response, accompanied by effective questioning on the part of the teacher, will afford opportunities for retrieval practice. In Chapter 1 we explored how retrieval practice is another well-evidenced strategy for ensuring that structural knowledge embeds in long-term memory.

Every few weeks I spend 20 minutes at the start of a class modelling a response to a GCSE task. On occasion this can cause a slight internal conflict, as within the constraints of a time-bound and content-heavy specification I feel I should be getting on with the teaching. However, while it may appear to slow down the learning process, it is highly probable that effective modelling will aid long-term retention and transfer. In the context of MFL, it has the potential to enhance the range of students' language and improve accuracy.

1. Deconstruction Modelling

Deconstructing or 'breaking down' a model answer with students in the MFL classroom enables them to observe not just the exact ingredients which go into the finished product, but also the balance needed to ensure as perfect an end outcome as possible. Typically, for GCSE Higher Writing, the 'ingredients' may include items such as:

♦ An advanced array of topic-related vocabulary.

♦ Opinions which are justified.

♦ Variety of subject pronouns and accurate conjugation.

♦ Variety of tenses and moods (present, perfect, imperfect, future subjunctive, etc.).

♦ Connectives and subordinate clauses.

♦ Idiomatic expressions.

For the purpose of deconstruction, it may be the case that the model is prepared in advance. This has a potential benefit in that it allows for the creation of a bespoke model which can be written to reflect the nuances of the class in question. For example, if the topic was 'free time and sport', and if fifteen of my eighteen-strong class were undertaking the Duke of Edinburgh's Award, I might choose this activity as exemplar content in my model. Additionally, models prepared in advance allow us to predict and address where misconceptions and mistakes may arise. If I know that some of the class have struggled with the structure of reflexive verbs in the past, I might build this into my model to allow for explicit referral and further exposure – for example, 'Je me suis bronzé(e)' or 'Nous nous sommes bien amusé(e)s'.

Before undertaking deconstruction of a model, it is worthwhile asking the students what they think would constitute an excellent response to a task. If they have knowledge of mark schemes, it may be worth reminding them to align their answers to them as far as possible. For a written task which asks students to outline why holidays are important and to describe a memorable holiday, the teacher might expect them to come up with the following:

Content

♦ Opinions and justification on holidays (relaxing/time with friends and family/broadening culture/perfecting a language/seeing new places).

♦ Description of a memorable holiday (information on travel/accommodation/facilities/weather/activities/a specific event).

♦ Plans for a future holiday or an ideal holiday.

Range of language

♦ Use of connectives and subordinate clauses.

♦ Different subject pronouns and accurate conjugation.

♦ Range of tenses.

This exercise in pre-empting excellence also reinforces with students the need for planning. Some teachers encourage students to use acronyms such as PROFS (see Chapter 2) during the planning stage in order to frame aspects of their responses.

When deconstructing a model, it may also be beneficial to offer students a narrative which describes the reason for some of the decisions you have taken in your writing as means of emphasising good practice. A task on 'free-time activities', for example, might go something like this:

In this sentence I was going to write 'j'ai joué au rugby', but as I had already used the verb 'jouer' twice, I wanted to vary my verb use and therefore I chose 'j'ai fait de l'escalade'.

Below is a model that I wrote for a recent piece of written work undertaken by my Year 11 class.

Write a response to the questions below.

1 Describe your daily routine:

Je me réveille à sept heures. Je me lève tout de suite et je me lave dans la salle de bains. Quinze minutes plus tard, je prends mon petit-déjeuner dans la cuisine avec ma famille. Nous mangeons d'habitude des céréales et du pain grillé, et je bois du jus d'orange. Ensuite je m'habille dans ma chambre en écoutant de la musique. Pendant la semaine, il faut que je mette mon uniforme scolaire. Je porte une chemise blanche, une cravate à rayures, une veste, un pantalon, des chaussures noires et des chaussettes grises. J'aime l'uniforme parce que tout le monde se ressemble. Par contre, on ne peut pas montrer son individualité. Puis je quitte la maison à huit heures et quart pour aller à l'école. Après le collège, je me détends en regardant la télé avec mon frère. J'aime bien les émissions de sport, parce que je suis une personne assez sportive. Je fais mes devoirs avant de me coucher. Je vais au lit à onze heures et demie. Demain je me lèverai de bonne heure parce que je dois réviser des maths. Dans un monde idéal, on pourrait faire la grasse matinée tous les jours!

I get up at 7am. I get up immediately and I wash in the bathroom. Fifteen minutes later, I have breakfast in the kitchen with my family. We normally eat cereal and toast, and I drink orange juice. Next I get dressed in my bedroom while listening to music. During the week, I have to put on a school uniform. I wear a white shirt, a stripy tie, a blazer, trousers, black shoes and grey socks. I like the uniform because everyone looks the same. On the other hand, you can't express your own identity. Then I leave the house at 8.15am to go to school. After school, I relax by watching TV with my brother. I really like sports programmes because I am quite a sporty person. I do my homework before going to bed. I go to bed at 11.30pm. Tomorrow I will get up early because I have to revise maths. In an ideal world, you could lie in every day of the week!

2   Describe what sports and leisure activities you undertake:

Samedi matin je joue au rugby pour mon lycée. Je m'en-traîne deux fois par semaine, mardi matin avant les cours, et jeudi après-midi. J'adore les sports collectifs, parce qu'on s'entraîne avec ses amis. En été je joue normalement au cricket et au badminton. De temps en temps je fais de la natation au centre sportif. Je me passionne pour les sports nautiques, comme la plongée sous-marine, bien que ce soit assez dangereuse. Je m'intéresse aussi aux films, surtout les films d'horreur. Mon film préféré s'appelle Dracula. *Ça me fait peur! Le weekend dernier, je suis allé au cinéma avec mes copains. Nous avons vu un film d'épouvante avec un acteur très célèbre. C'était effrayant! Ensuite nous avons dîné ensemble au restaurant. J'ai commandé du poulet rôti avec des frites. Après avoir mangé, nous sommes rentrés chez moi pour jouer à l'ordinateur. Nous nous sommes bien amusé(e)s.*

On Saturday mornings I play rugby for my school. I train twice a week, on Tuesday mornings before lessons and Thursday afternoons. I love team sports because you train with friends. In summer I normally play cricket and badminton. From time to time I swim at the sports centre. I am passionate about water sports, like deep-sea diving, although it is quite dangerous. I'm also interested in films, particularly horror films. My favourite film is called *Dracula*. It scares me! Last weekend, I went to the cinema with my mates. We saw a horror film with a very famous actor in it. It was frightening! Then we all had dinner together in a restaurant. I ordered the roast chicken with chips. After eating, we went back to my house to play on the computer. We had a great time.

As a starter activity, I may give students some time to work in pairs to decide how the model may meet the top band description from appropriate mark schemes. As such, the students might ask themselves the following questions.

Content

♦ How is the answer relevant to the question?

♦ How is the answer detailed? How does it convey a lot of information?

♦ How are opinions expressed and justified?

Range of language

♦ How does it demonstrate a range of vocabulary?

♦ How are structures used? How are various tenses attempted?

Accuracy

♦ Is the answer mostly accurate or are there errors?

♦ Do these errors hinder communication?

♦ Are verb tenses accurate?

Whole-class feedback will give the students an opportunity to justify their judgements, potentially from well-defined teacher questioning which orients their attention to excellence:

♦ How many daily routine phrases are mentioned in the first response ... James?

♦ Can you find an example of how the writer has changed pronoun use from 'je' to a different pronoun, perhaps to display his knowledge of verb conjugation ... Leila?

♦ How do we know that the writer is a boy (use of 'sportif' instead of 'sportive') ... Robbie?

- Can you find an example of how synonyms have been used effectively in this answer ('normalement'/'d'habitude', 'puis/ensuite', 'un film d'horreur'/'un film d'épouvante', 'effrayant'/'ça me fait peur') ... Shannon?

- Can you find me an example of a present participle ... Nadura?

- Can you find examples of high-level use of vocabulary ... Elise?

- How many examples of reflexive pronouns can you find ... Jessica?

- Read out for me an example of a justified opinion ... Siobhan.

- Locate for me examples of adjectival agreement ... Richard.

- Can you find me examples of the following tenses:
  ◊ Présent
  ◊ Passé composé
  ◊ Futur simple
  ◊ Futur proche
  ◊ Conditionnel

- Find me an example of the subjunctive mood ... Jack.

Naturally, you do not have to wait until the students have completed the course in order to deconstruct a model. If we are expecting our Year 7 students to write extended answers in our lessons, tests and exams, then there is scope for deconstructing a model from the earliest stages. From the moment they begin their language learning journey, effective modelling allows us to reinforce strong expectations with regard to the use of high-level vocabulary and variety of language.

At the simplest level, this may involve encouraging our Year 7 students to vary and broaden their range of vocabulary as they write. In response to a question about what is in their school bag, for example, instead of just writing three items of vocabulary, they could consider writing three things in their bag and three things in their pencil case, and then three things they don't have. Instead of just three items of vocabulary, all of a sudden they are using nine! As they develop their linguistic schemata, models could increasingly incorporate vocabulary, structures and forms taught some time previously, thus reinforcing the desirable difficulties of spacing, interleaving and offering prime opportunities for retrieval.

2. Live Modelling

While deconstruction equates to working backwards from a finished model, live modelling involves working forwards by writing a model 'live' in the classroom. This can be constructed either by the teacher and discussed with the students, or the students can play an active role in decisions regarding the construction of the model (co-construction). This allows for a very clear and explicit discussion of the processes that lead to excellence. This can be done by typing up a model with the class, although I prefer handwriting it on the board or via a visualiser. I find that it takes a little longer to type accents (unless you have accents assigned to shortcut keys or are aware of other shortcuts) and the predictive element of programs such as Microsoft Word will sometimes change words if it is not set to the language in question (e.g. 'cinéma' suddenly becomes 'cinema'). This leads to wasted time.

Live modelling allows for discussion on how and why we are writing in the way we are. It also facilitates editing, refining and even the correction of mistakes. These are all important aspects of the aforementioned thought processes. For instance, to return to the rugby example, a potential discussion when co-constructing with the class may go something like this:

We have used rugby as the sport in this sentence; however, that is now the second activity we have used which is a cognate. Perhaps we need to review this and amend the activity to reflect the more advanced vocabulary we want to display. Can anyone think of a more preferable option?

Or:

We have written here 'il faut jouer à un sport pour garder la forme'. While this is correct, perhaps the use of 'pratiquer un sport' may be a better option stylistically.

This type of co-construction also allows for 'machine-gun' modelling, whereby the teacher asks students quick-fire questions during the process. This not only affords an opportunity for retrieval practice but also clears up misconceptions.

Can you give me three non-cognate sports which use the verb 'faire' ... Usain?

Can you think how we might build in 'être' as an auxiliary verb in the perfect tense ... Rachel?

How might we justify a positive opinion on swimming ... Lucy?

Thinking of PROFS, we are still missing a subjunctive in our model. Can you think of a potential example ... Max?

When constructing or deconstructing a model before the students complete their own task, it may be prudent to ensure that the target product is slightly different from the modelled task. We don't want our students to simply regurgitate the model or modify it in a superficial manner – for example, 'me gusta el fútbol' becomes 'me gusta el rugby'! After all, one of our aims is to ensure that they can transfer modelled excellence into slightly different contexts.

There may also be times when you wish to model after the students have completed the task. This is particularly useful in ensuring the students have a benchmark of excellence against which they can compare their own work and consequently refine accordingly. Whenever I do this in my own classroom, I often request that the students learn aspects of their refined work by heart (e.g. their PROFS structures), as the automaticity of these structures in long-term memory can be highly valuable.

3. Admire Others

You may wish to consider using models created by others. This can have benefits on a number of levels. For example, if you are fortunate enough to have access to a foreign language assistant, you may be able to invite him/her as an authentic 'expert' to create a model for deconstruction with the class. This will certainly enhance and promote authenticity in language use, although it will also require careful unpicking with the class.

Another strategy is to use the work of past students. My own department has recalled the GCSE exam scripts of students who have performed at a high level for use as models (with their permission, of course). Our students will most likely relate to a model which has been created by a peer, and if the model sets the bar high they may feel more inclined to believe that they can emulate it. You can also compare these authentic exam scripts with teacher-created models. Students normally like to seek reasons for justifying why the student model is better!

There is also great scope for modelling student work from within the class. I find this particularly useful when focusing on one aspect of language use, such as the use of a tense or subordinating conjunctions in German. This may involve using a visualiser to model the students' work live and high-lighting the aspect in question or taking a picture of their work as they write and displaying it on the board. Doug Lemov refers to 'Show Call' as: "a type of Cold Call that involves taking students' written work and displaying it to the class. Champion teachers use it to maximize rigor and accountability for written work, spotlight 'bright spots' in student work, and build a culture of revision."[1]

---

1   See http://teachlikeachampion.com/plugandplay/showcall.

A typical discussion with the class during this phase may sound something like:

Look at how Matthew has employed a subordinating conjunction in his work: "Deutsch gefällt mir, obwohl die Grammatik schwer ist." Let's not forget that subordinating conjunctions will enrich our work and earn us marks for range of language and accuracy. Can anyone remind me of other subordinating conjunctions in German?

Such a technique is useful not only because it benchmarks brilliance by peers for peers, but also because it helps to harness students' working memory. When we are teaching in our classrooms, students are operating primarily from their working memory. The problem is that working memory is a bottleneck that is fixed, restricted and easily overloaded. Ideally, therefore, our students should be able to draw on knowledge from long-term memory in order to ease the cognitive load on working memory.

It is up to us as teachers to create the right conditions in our classrooms to harness working memory. One such strategy is to orient students' attention to the specific aspect of learning you wish them to focus on. Peps Mccrea expounds on this in his book *Memorable Teaching*: "If we want to control what our students learn, we've got to be intentional and specific about what they should be attending to. Not only do we need to orient attention, but we must do it with precision."[2]

When I need to address and improve students' ability to manipulate and produce a very specific aspect of language, such as a structure, conjugation or tense usage, I find the 'Show Call' strategy highly effective in orienting their attention – either at the start or during the course of the lesson.

---

2   Peps Mccrea, *Memorable Teaching: Leveraging Memory to Build Deep and Durable Learning in the Classroom* (n.p.: CreateSpace, 2017), p. 41.

4. Comparing Models

Comparing models can be highly effective in guiding students towards excellence. For example, contrasting a high-quality model with a low-quality model allows for the reinforcement of mark scheme criteria against content, range of language and accuracy. It is important to steer students as they tease out specific judgements, otherwise their assessment of the differences between the models may be too simplistic and superficial – for example, "Model A is more accurate."

A strategy I find particularly useful is to then provide students with two models which are much more similar in terms of quality – each with specific strengths, weaknesses and areas for improvement. This allows for a really deep discussion with the students about the intricacies of advanced language use in written responses. Most exam boards will typically provide such models as part of their support to schools.

Consider these two responses to a Spanish question which asked students to write a message to a Spanish friend about holidays, saying where they went last year, with whom they go on holiday, their ideal holiday and opinions on tourism.

---

1. *El año pasado fui a Salou con mi familia y lo pasamos muy bien porque hizo un tiempo mucho mejor que en Irlanda del Norte.*

   Generalmente voy de vacaciones con mis amigos, pero preferirían ir con mi familia porque son menos aburridos. Para mis vacaciones ideales iría a Kenia porque me interesa naturaleza. Me gustaría visitar todos los sitios de interés con mis amigos.

   En mi opinión, el turismo es importante para un país porque ayuda la economía y crea empleos. Sin embargo hay muchas desventajas también.

2. *El año pasado fui a Japón con mis amigos. Fue muy divertido porque tomar al sol y fuimos de compras. Como comida de español como sushi, fue muy delisioso pero no me gusta pescado.*

   Para mis ideales vacaciones quieo ir a Suiza porque hablo francés y alemán tambien es bastante calor en Suiza y quiero caminar en las montañas, espero que tomía al sol.

   Creo que el turismo es importante porque a muchas personas les gusta el buen clima y gastan dinero mucho en las tiendas.

Strengths

♦ Both responses cover the required information.

♦ The information is communicated effectively in the target language.

♦ Attempts at justifying opinions are generally successful.

Weaknesses

♦ Some errors, mostly minor, including word order, missing definite articles and incorrect conjugation.

♦ Some unnecessary repetition.

Each offers its own strengths, mistakes and areas for development. The advantage of unpicking comparable models of a similar quality can provide a rich mine of dos and don'ts which can inform and guide student improvement.

5. Modelling Speaking

While we might naturally think of writing when we consider the rationale for and impact of modelling in the MFL classroom, there are of course two productive skills which require student output: writing and speaking. It is therefore worthwhile to consider some approaches to modelling speaking in our lessons. Invariably, this will be for the purpose of ensuring accuracy in pronunciation.

♦ MFL teachers know the benefit of repetition and drill when trying to perfect pronunciation. The 'I say, you say' strategy for modelling individual words or phrases with individuals or with the whole class allows for the immediate rehearsal of speaking between expert and novice. If a student mispronounces a word within a phrase or structure, it is better to correct it rather than let it go unchecked – in the same way that we would correct inaccurate spelling in written work. Recently I have also observed good use of drill, during which a teacher said a phrase in English and the class chanted it back in French. Phrases were then extended until full sentences and mini paragraphs were being recited. If there was any inaccuracy or hesitation, the phrase was repeated and rehearsed until it was perfect. I even know of one teacher who, rather than waiting for the whole class to enter, starts this process immediately when one or two students have arrived in the room; the others join in with the drill process as they arrive. Drill and repetition – when spaced and interleaved – may enhance student automaticity of structures. An example might be:

Teacher: *Répétez: J'habite …*

Class: *J'habite …*

Teacher: *Comment dit-on 'in a house' … Jonny?*

Jonny: *… dans une maison.*

Teacher: *Répétez: J'habite dans une maison …*

Class: *J'habite dans une maison …*

Teacher: *Comment dit-on 'in the countryside' … Claire?*

Claire: *… à la campagne.*

Teacher: *Répétez: J'habite dans une maison à la campagne.*

Class: *J'habite dans une maison à la campagne.*

Teacher: *Comment dit-on 'with my friends' … Raymond?*

Raymond: *… avec mes copains.*

Teacher: *Répétez: J'habite dans une maison à la campagne avec mes copains.*

Class: *J'habite dans une maison à la campagne avec mes copains.*

♦ If there is the opportunity for student work to be recorded, this is also an attractive option. Students can be encouraged to listen to the recordings at frequent intervals and pause when appropriate for repetition or rehearsal.

♦ There are many websites which include quite accurate pronunciation of language for the purposes of modelling. One of my favourites is Quizlet (https://quizlet.com), which affords teachers the opportunity to create language quizzes to aid student retrieval practice. Students can also listen to the language being tested to enhance their spoken accuracy.

♦ Some schools adopt frameworks such as CUDDLES to help with the perfection of spoken accuracy. While this involves the annotation of written models, it has a specific emphasis on enhancing spoken accuracy. For example, words in French which have a silent ending have their last letter underlined with dots. If there is liaison and the 's' at the end of the word is pronounced, there will be an underscore to link the word with the next – for example:

Je préfère les chats parce qu'ils sont plus indépendants.

The following explanation of CUDDLES is adapted from Jess Lund's blog post:

C – count the number of letters in each word. *This is particularly pertinent when beginners are learning high-frequency words – for example, 'Je n'ai pas de ...' (2/1'2/3/2).*

U – underline the vowel combinations. *Vowel sounds are a key lever in pronunciation. If students know early on that 'oi' in French makes a 'wa' sound, over time they come to read 'oi' as 'wa' automatically.*

D – double underline the double consonants. *This helps to focus students' attention on the spelling and sound of the word at the same time.*

D – dot the silent letters. *This helps students to increase authenticity in their spoken language. For example, if they know that in French '-ment' is pronounced 'mon' and is the equivalent of the English suffix '-ly', suddenly the pronunciation of 'normalement', 'suffisamment', 'malheureusement', 'heureusement' and 'rarement' becomes 'un jeu d'enfant'.*

L – mark the liaisons. *This can have a big impact on pronunciation and authenticity.*

E – exaggerate your accents. *Exaggerating the size of accents not only draws students' attention to their presence and ensures that they think about the pronunciation of the resulting word, but it can also help them to remember the pronunciation and spelling of words.*

S – stories. *These are particularly useful to help with the spelling of words, including mnemonics. Sometimes the sillier, the better! For example: M'APPELLE – Mary and Peter's planted pineapples eventually looked like eggplants.[3]*

In my own classes, we spend some time from Year 7 onwards annotating written work using the CUDDLES approach, including knowledge organiser sentences which follow the PROFS format. Examples of sentences which my Year 7 class have annotated using the CUDDLES approach for the topic of 'house and home' include:

♦ *Hier soir, j'ai dîné avec ma famille.*

   Last night I had dinner with my family.

♦ *J'ai toujours partagé une chambre avec mon frère.*

   I have always shared a bedroom with my brother.

♦ *Je me dispute avec ma sœur car elle est très gâtée.*

   I argue with my sister because she is very spoiled.

♦ *J'adore ma maison parce qu'elle est grande, confortable et moderne.*

   I love my house because it's big, comfortable and modern.

♦ *J'aime beaucoup avoir ma propre chambre car j'ai beaucoup de place pour toutes mes affaires.*

   I really like having my own room because I have a lot of space for all my things.

---

3   Lund, Aides-mémoire.

♦ *Ma maison idéale serait énorme avec une piscine et un court de tennis.*

My ideal house would be enormous with a swimming pool and a tennis court.

♦ *Samedi prochain je vais passer la journée avec mes parents.*

Next Saturday I am going to spend the day with my parents.

♦ *À l'avenir j'espère vivre dans une grande ville.*

In the future I hope to live in a big city.

♦ *Il faut que je range ma chambre une fois par semaine.*

I must tidy my room once a week.

♦ *Je m'entends bien avec mon père bien qu'il soit assez strict.*

I get on well with my dad even though he is quite strict.

Often, following annotation using the CUDDLES approach, we rehearse and practise phrases. I will read out the annotated sentence and they repeat it. Following much repetition, and as phrases start to embed in long-term memory, I will say a phrase in English and they will repeat it in the target language. The use of strategies such as CUDDLES has the potential to make their written and spoken language not just more accurate but also more authentic.

Reflective Questions

♦ Do you think about whether to deconstruct a pre-prepared model or co-construct live with the class? If deconstructing, do you give the students a narrative of your thought processes as you wrote it? If constructing live, do you involve students in the decision-making, allowing for drafting, editing and the correction of mistakes?

- Do you question the students as you construct the model, encouraging retrieval practice and the reinforcement of expectations in writing?

- Do you consider whether to model before or after the students complete the task?

- Do you compare models in order to heighten the students' awareness and understanding of high standards?

- Do you model students' own work in order to orient attention and to share and celebrate peer success as a further reflection of expected standards?

Chapter 4
Practice

Ella's class in Year 9 have just finished the topic of 'holidays', in which they reviewed country vocabulary, learnt how to construct phrases to say how they travelled, retrieved weather phrases, talked and wrote about a broad range of holiday activities using the structure 'on peut', gave and justified opinions on accommodation types, learnt the futur proche as a tense and acquired cultural information on French-speaking countries. Ella's teacher, Miss Holmes, then set the class a written activity to complete under exam conditions in which they were required to bring together all the strands of the aforementioned learning into a coherent paragraph in the target language.

Despite feeling that she had grasped the concepts and content during lessons, Ella struggled when she was asked to combine them accurately into a written response from memory. She was not surprised, therefore, on receiving the marked response, to find Miss Holmes' corrections strewn throughout her work in green pen. For example, Ella had not conjugated the verb 'aller' correctly in the futur proche and had failed to follow the verb 'aller' with infinitives to construct the tense correctly. On occasions she had also mistakenly placed the pronoun 'je' after 'on peut' and before the infinitive when describing holiday activities. There were further inaccuracies in spelling. Ella feels somewhat deflated at the outcome and is at a loss to identify with certainty why the outcome was not better, given her enjoyment of the topic and her sense that she was understanding the material. She vows to ask Miss Holmes what she needs to do to improve next time.

Many of the issues encountered by Ella in this example may ultimately refer back to a lack of practice. Put simply, practice matters a great deal. While we can explain and model very effectively, if it is not backed up by robust practice the students' learning may be impeded. As Daisy Christodoulou outlines in her book *Making Good Progress?*, practice is absolutely vital for skill development. If we want our students to become highly skilled linguists, we must afford them as many opportunities as possible to practise and master linguistic concepts.[1]

Of course, the ultimate practice for any aspiring linguist must surely be immersing themselves in the target language and culture, ideally through visiting or even living in a target language country for a period of time. This presents them not only with opportunities to use linguistic knowledge already stored in long-term memory, but also to interact in a manner which allows for the negotiation of meaning, for clarification, for understanding and for a deeper understanding of cultural nuances such as dialects and pronunciation variances. Before I travelled abroad to spend a gap year in Germany many years ago, my teacher told me that I would know I had 'made it' in the language when I started to dream in German. While cognitive science may not yet be so advanced that it can explore the correlation and causality between dream state and long-term memory, the

---

1   Christodoulou, *Making Good Progress?*, p. 48.

romantic linguist in me likes to think that there may be some truth in this adage! However, my proudest moment, rather ironically, came after an eye operation some months after my year abroad when the nurse was able to tell me that I had 'rambled on at length' in German when coming out of anaesthesia!

Within the constraints of a timetabled curriculum, when our students may only grace our classrooms two or three times per week for short bursts of teaching, such immersion experiences are clearly not possible. However, the main, overarching long-term goals of practice in the MFL classroom should surely be as follows:

♦ To ensure that linguistic knowledge, forms and structures are so well embedded in long-term memory that they can be effortlessly recalled or performed once mastered. In other words, they become automatic.

♦ To develop and deepen students' receptive and productive skills: listening, reading, speaking and writing.

♦ To give our students opportunities to interact in the target language for the purpose of comprehending input and modifying their own outputs, and to develop their skills in negotiating meaning so they can seek clarification, check for understanding, take ownership in addressing and bridging any gaps in knowledge, and modify their own spoken and written outputs accordingly.

We will explore the latter point in Chapter 6, but the remainder of this chapter will focus on how deliberate practice in our classrooms can meet the aspirations outlined in the first two points above. Both points are very much interrelated, as well-designed listening, reading, speaking and writing practice can, of course, facilitate and expedite the process of embedding and reinforcing core knowledge in long-term memory.

In relation to the first point, it is perhaps useful to think about what exactly we want our students to consolidate well in long-term memory, as they journey from beginner to expert, in order for it to become automatic. This may be multilayered:

♦ Grammatical and linguistic forms, structures and rules.

♦ Learnt sentences aimed at exemplifying a structure.

♦ Increasingly advanced examples of functional language, such as giving preferences.

♦ Lexical banks, most pertinently high-frequency words.

♦ Idiomatic expressions unique to the target language.

The above list may determine our approach to practice in the classroom. Moreover, if we employ classroom practice effectively it will help to ensure that student outputs in the language are not just perfect in terms of accuracy, but permanent in relation to their automaticity in long-term memory.

It is important that we do not overlook the importance of practice in favour of 'moving on quickly', reflective of the rush and clamour approach to the curriculum in England. This is dangerous, as sustained practice is essential if students are to master the language. In his renowned paper on the 'Principles of Instruction', Barak Rosenshine conveys clearly as his second principle the importance of presenting material in small steps with (guided) student practice after each step.[2] He suggests that the most effective maths teachers spend approximately 23 minutes of a 40-minute lesson in what John Hattie would refer to as 'direct instruction' – explaining, modelling, giving worked examples, guiding practice and checking for student understanding.[3] The least effective spent approximately 11 minutes on this. Thus, the principles of explaining, modelling and questioning are all

---

2   Rosenshine, Principles of Instruction, p. 13.
3   John Hattie, *Visible Learning: A Synthesis of 800 Meta-Analyses Relating to Achievement* (New York: Routledge, 2009).

intertwined with that of practice. In fact, to use an analogy from the original *Making Every Lesson Count* book – if challenge, explaining, modelling and questioning are the ingredients for learning, practice is the oven in which it is baked.[4] Without robust practice, our students risk falling between the rungs of the ladder they are attempting to climb in their learning. If we build opportunities for them to practise in our lessons, and if we use it to check their understanding effectively, not only will it allow us to respond to misconceptions which arise in their learning, but it will also play its part in developing their ability to work independently as they journey towards fluency in the language. Therefore, it is much better to overcook in the oven than undercook!

So what should practice look like in our classrooms? Rosenshine's principle of breaking new material into small steps with student practice after each step is expounded on further by Daisy Christodoulou. In *Making Good Progress?* she discusses the 'knowing-doing gap' – the notion that our students know what they are supposed to do, yet don't do it reliably.[5] She gives the example of capital letters in English. The vast majority of students know they must use capital letters at the start of sentences, but fewer students consistently do so. In modern foreign languages, we can perhaps think of similar examples. In German, our students may know that the verb reverts to the end of the sentence after 'obwohl', but fewer students will do so consistently. The answer to the knowing-doing gap for Christodoulou lies in deliberate practice – namely, the isolation and practice of the particular sub-skill we want students to be able to do. In the case of subordinate conjunctions in German, this may involve getting them to write out sentences with 'obwohl', asking them to identify the five mistakes in a series of ten sentences with subordinating conjunctions, and getting

---

4   Allison and Tharby, *Making Every Lesson Count*, p. 129.
5   Christodoulou, *Making Good Progress?*, p. 49.

them to write a short paragraph using subordinate clauses based on stimuli.

In our teaching, the small constituent parts which comprise deliberate practice may look very different from the final skill. Let's take Ella's work as an example. The final skill was to write a high-level GCSE-style paragraph on the topic of holidays. However, what was probably lacking to a certain extent in lessons was the deliberate practice after material had been broken down into small steps. Potential deliberate and focused practice for Ella may have included:

♦ Conjugation of the verb 'aller' to describe what means of transport people use to arrive at holiday destinations.

♦ The use of 'aller' with infinitives in order to structure the futur proche.

♦ The use of 'on peut' with infinitives as a structure.

♦ Sentence starters for giving opinions (e.g. *Je trouve que … , Je pense que … , Je crois que … , À mon avis … , Selon moi … , J'adore … , Je préfère …*).

♦ The use of connectives when giving and justifying opinions.

These discrete component parts look very different from the final product, just like spending focused and deliberate time practising the dribbling of a basketball is very different from playing a full-blown match against an opposing team, but is a necessity in order to master the game. This type of deliberate practice not only ensures that working memory is not overloaded by tasks being too complex, but it also allows for feedback to be very precise because tasks are more specific.

This does not mean that deliberate practice should be easy or undertaken within a student's comfort zone. If anything, deliberate practice must be challenging. In Ella's example, the deliberate practice of the conjugation of 'aller' may involve its usage not just within sentences on the topic of holidays, but also in a range of transferable contexts. It may include a requirement for students to conjugate the verb using a given pronoun or using proper nouns. Students tend to struggle with the latter:

Il _____ *en vacances en hiver.* (conjugation with pronoun)

Sasha et moi _____ *ensemble en Espagne au mois d'août.* (conjugation with a proper noun included)

The potential that deliberate practice affords in guiding student practice and monitoring student understanding cannot be overestimated. If we subscribe to the theory of Doug Lemov, Erica Woolway and Katie Yezzi in *Practice Perfect* that 'practice makes permanent' rather than perfect, then the use of worked examples, assisting and guiding practice, and checking for understanding during and following practice all play key roles in determining that our students will not fall into bad habits in their use of language, whether stylistically, grammatically or otherwise.[6] In fact, the balance between assisted practice and the amount of independent thinking the teacher expects during practice should be a key concern in our pursuit of meaningful practice. As Allison and Tharby explain in the original *Making Every Lesson Count* book, the ratio will shift along a spectrum from dependency to independence as students become more confident and fluent in new material.[7]

In some lessons they will be at the dependency stage of the direct instruction model, listening to explanations and working with models. As they undertake deliberate practice, they will be at the heavy guidance or light guidance stage, possibly doing worked examples or using well-crafted writing frames in order to practise a specific component with regular teacher feedback. In other lessons, they will be working at the autonomy stage, utilising their linguistic

---

6   Doug Lemov, Erica Woolway and Katie Yezzi, *Practice Perfect: 42 Rules for Getting Better at Getting Better* (San Francisco, CA: Jossey-Bass, 2018), p. 25.

7   See Allison and Tharby, *Making Every Lesson Count*, p. 127.

knowledge and skill in order to produce a coherent end outcome, often made up of component parts, as in Ella's
example. At this stage they will hopefully be manipulating
and 'owning' the language for their own purposes. As might
be expected, the journey from dependency to autonomy may
vary depending on the difficulty of material and the class in
front of us. It is our job to decide when students have had
enough practice to move on.

The remainder of this chapter will look at strategies for
facilitating practice, as well as undertaking practice in the
classroom.

1. Knowledge Organisers

Knowledge organisers allow us to put all the core knowledge we want our students to practise in one place. The
benefits of this are numerous:

♦ They act as a road map, demonstrating clearly for students where they are and where the cumulative build-up
  of knowledge will take them over the year.

♦ If done properly, they facilitate strong self-quizzing techniques and retrieval practice, which in turn expedite the consolidation of knowledge into long-term memory.

♦ They have the potential to reduce cognitive load when knowledge becomes automatic.

Perhaps, unlike disciplines such as history and science, determining what 'factual knowledge' looks like in the modern foreign languages classroom is a trickier prospect. And this is where we need to be careful: some knowledge organisers seem to be nothing more than vocabulary lists. While vocabulary knowledge is important, of course, this limitation is potentially dangerous. A knowledge-based approach must go hand in hand with the highest of expectations and aspirations for our students' learning.

Knowledge organisers should assist us with the process of giving students the declarative and procedural knowledge which, in time, will allow them to make connections, transfer meaning and manipulate language effectively at a high level, utilising the complex interplay between environment, long-term memory and working memory. Knowledge organisers which require our students to embed exemplars of structures and styles in long-term memory, through the PROFS approach (as seen in Chapter 2) or other techniques, enable them to make connections and patterns which will deepen their learning when they are explicitly taught the structures and allow them to 'chunk' structures in long-term memory.

Here are some potential tips for creating knowledge organisers for MFL:

♦ As a department, map out the core knowledge and cultural capital you want your students to gain over the key stage. What core concepts and structures do your students need to have mastered by the end of the key stage in order to prepare them effectively for what comes next?

♦ Think about how the knowledge base should build cumulatively as students progress through the key stage.

♦ Organise the knowledge under clear headings. Don't try to cram too much into a knowledge organiser. If necessary, make a number of knowledge organisers to cover the knowledge you want the students to acquire.

♦ Ensure the students can access them quickly. They may be stuck into books or in a separate folder. Have spare copies to hand.

♦ Refer to them regularly in lessons. If your knowledge organisers contain extended structures, spend time with the students rehearsing them, repeating them and drilling them in an explicit manner.

♦ Reinforce through frequent and regular self-quizzing. Ensure the students are spending time outside of the classroom self-quizzing against their knowledge organiser as a means of retrieval practice. Get them to follow three steps for self-quizzing:

    1 Read over the relevant knowledge for a period of time.

    2 Write down what you remember.

    3 Check what you have written against your knowledge organiser and correct in a different coloured pen, if necessary.

♦ Assist the quizzing aspect of knowledge organisers by creating pared down versions (e.g. ones with missing vocabulary or key words). These can also be very good for revision.

♦ Explicitly emphasise the correlation between self-quizzing and effective revision strategies. Those who self-quiz effectively as a revision technique are likely to perform better in exams.

2. Retrieval Practice

Retrieval practice, put very simply, is the act of trying to recall information without having it in front of you. Study upon study indicates that the way to counter this is when we ask students to retrieve from memory after a period of time – after a few days, weeks or months. And if we return to the same knowledge repeatedly and in a spaced out manner (with increasingly long gaps over time), we are expediting the potential for real learning.

Retrieval practice must be frequent and spaced, a point which is emphasised by Peter Brown, Henry Roediger and Mark McDaniel: "Practicing retrieval makes learning stick far better than reexposure to the original material does. To be most effective, retrieval must be repeated again and again, in spaced out sessions so that the recall, rather than becoming a mindless recitation, requires some cognitive effort."[8]

To be most effective, retrieval practice must also be relevant. It must be very tightly bound to the core knowledge outlined in the knowledge organiser or other curriculum content map, and the most effective retrieval practice will prepare students for new knowledge they are about to encounter.

In Rosenshine's 'Principles of Instruction', weekly and monthly recap in the classroom are identified as an integral part of effective teaching.[9] These short recap sessions, which

---

8   Brown et al., p. 28.
9   Rosenshine, Principles of Instruction, p. 19.

last five–ten minutes, are low stakes, frequent and challenging. They are challenging because the students are starting to forget (or have forgotten) material from the previous lesson and because the retrieval is 'spaced', so they are also being asked to recall knowledge from a few weeks, months or even years ago. This is taxing, but essential if it is to embed in long-term memory. A common strategy my own school uses is a short quiz sheet on which the students translate words and phrases into English and then into the target language. Sometimes they are asked to conjugate verbs or to explain a grammatical rule. The teachers aim to write the retrieval practice quiz so that it is challenging but will also allow most of the students to experience some success. If students are getting 70–75% that is a good rule of thumb. Success which is borne from challenge most likely enhances motivation. Tellingly, only rarely does a student get full marks. They find it tough but hopefully rewarding.

While retrieval practice should be consistent in terms of frequency, there is perhaps scope for varying its delivery to maintain the momentum of challenge. Here are some examples of retrieval practice concepts for use at the start of lessons:

- A 'do-now' challenge which requires students to retrieve vocabulary, conjugate from memory, find the odd one out or translate.

- A 'five-a-day' challenge in which students must conjugate, list (e.g. adjectives on a topic), spot the odd one out, correct a mistake or translate a sentence.

- A 'boggle activity' whereby students are required to retrieve and spell as many words as possible on a theme based on sixteen or so given letters.

- A 'Connect 4' theme in which students must translate four words in separate discs of the same colour.

♦ A knowledge retrieval challenge whereby students get one point for the retrieval of a word/phrase from the last lesson, two points for last week's lesson, three points for last month's lesson and four points for last year's lesson. An example from one of my own recent lessons appears below. Each row is colour coded depending on whether the words/phrases found within it relate to the last lesson, last week, last year or last month.

It's snowing	Budgie	Shirt	Last Year 4 Points
We do	Board games	Scuba diving	Last Month 3 Points
Traffic lights	Bakery	The beach	Last Week 2 Points
How do I get to the bank?	The first street on the right	as far as the corner	Last Lesson 1 Point

There is no doubt that technology has a place in the modern foreign languages classroom, particularly for practices that are backed up by cognitive science such as retrieval. One prominent site for MFL is Quizlet, which allows teachers to create quiz sets – very quickly and expediently – that can be employed for retrieval practice. If you prefer, they can be made solely on word or phrase recognition without the distractions of clip art. Once created, the students have a range of activities from which to choose. These types of well-designed and structured self-quizzing activities (with the principles of spacing and interleaving built in) serve to facilitate learning. Other sites worth exploring include Quizizz (www.quizizz.com) and Kahoot (www.kahoot.com). For all things related to technology in the MFL classroom, I would really recommend Joe Dale's excellent podcasts. Joe can be found on Twitter: @joedale, using #MFLtwitteratipodcast.

3. Go Micro

As discussed already in this chapter, deliberate practice in the MFL classroom will quite often look very different to the end product. If our goal is to get the students writing or speaking fluently about a given topic, such as their career choices and future plans, then it is important that we orient their attention towards the fine detail – the small blocks of knowledge which will build accumulatively towards the final goal. By focusing their attention in this way, through modelling and then through practice, we are likely to harness working memory in a manner which will enable them to embed structures in long-term memory. The intertwining of micro-modelling and micro-practice in this manner also enables students to return to structures at repeated intervals in order to facilitate the automaticity of such structures. The late Graham Nuthall discovered that in order to learn a new concept, a student must revisit it in its entirety at least three times over a few days or weeks.[10]

Let's look at a possible schedule for deliberate practice for the topic of career choices and future plans, with the end goal of writing an extended higher-level GCSE answer:

♦ Career vocabulary within the context of extended listening and reading exercises.

♦ Opinions and justification on job choices.

♦ Regular verbs future tense.

♦ Irregular verbs future tense.

♦ Conditional tense.

♦ Specific structures.

While the practice of grammatical structures may be rooted within the context at hand, notably careers and future plans, it is likely that we will want to build in practice of the structure within other contexts in order to embed challenge and deepen the students' understanding. As we have seen, the specific micro-practice may look very different from the end outcome, just like the aforementioned practice of basketball dribbling is very different to playing an entire game.

When such deliberate practice is accompanied and followed by modelling techniques, such as the deconstruction of a potential GCSE answer, it allows for a revisit of the component parts which will aid consolidation in long-term memory.

---

10 Graham Nuthall, *The Hidden Lives of Learners* (Wellington: New Zealand Council for Educational Research Press, 2007), p. 127.

4. Overlearn

For a new skill to become automatic or for new knowledge to become long-lasting, sustained practice beyond the point of mastery is necessary. As Daniel Willingham acknowledges, the unexpected finding from cognitive science is that practice does not make perfect.[11] Practise until you are perfect and you will be perfect only briefly. What is necessary is sustained practice. This means regular, ongoing review or the use of the target material.

In the MFL classroom, we must always ensure that curriculum planning builds in opportunities for students to *overlearn* – to practise beyond the point of mastery. For example, once the conditional tense has been explicitly taught and mastered through deliberate practice, such as in the example of 'career choices and future plans' on page 105, return to it within a different context some weeks later in order to provide opportunities to overlearn the structures and to manipulate them within a different context. In my own school's curriculum, 'career choices and future plans' is followed by 'environmental issues', so I would ensure that part of this topic gave students the chance to describe and depict their ideal world, thus allowing for further practice of the conditional and its manipulation. In this manner, we are also building in the desirable difficulties of spacing and interleaving which will ultimately help to embed structures in long-term memory.

---

11 Daniel Willingham, Practice Makes Perfect – But Only If You Practice Beyond the Point of Perfection, *American Educator* (spring 2004). Available at: https://www.aft.org/periodical/american-educator/spring-2004/ask-cognitive-scientist.

Skills-based practice

Practising listening, speaking, reading and writing skills discretely not only helps to hone them, but also plays a part in reinforcing core knowledge in long-term memory. While the previous chapter and upcoming chapters explore in some detail how writing skills may be developed and honed, the following sections on specific skills-based practice in listening, speaking and reading offer some principles and strategies for ensuring that this is also effective in our MFL classrooms. The suggestions are not exhaustive and are really just the tip of the iceberg. A weekly check of the #mfltwitterati feed will invariably throw up new, exciting and interesting strategies which are being trialled by many dedicated MFL teachers the length and breadth of the country.

Listening

There are a number of principles when undertaking listening practice which in my experience are worth embedding from the very start in a student's language learning experience:

♦ Ensure there is a pre- and post-listening phase.

♦ Orient their attention towards the purpose – what they need to be listening for and its importance.

♦ Emphasise that they do not need to understand every word in order to extrapolate the necessary information.

♦ Try to move from global understanding to detailed understanding; this may involve expanding the task brief to introduce more challenge.

♦ Take time to listen again and again should mishearing need to be rectified.

♦ Make the practice as active as possible.

Every year I undertake a particular listening activity on leisure activities from the textbook with my Year 8 class. Every year I forget to teach them the word for 'fishing' in advance of the task. Every year I figuratively kick myself in frustration when I hear the word come up on the CD. Every year my students get that answer wrong because they don't have the lexical knowledge.

When I'm organised, I check the transcripts to ensure there are no gaps in student knowledge before undertaking the task. Often, as part of a pre-listening activity, I would brainstorm with students likely lexical items which may come up in the listening task. If there are any new items which they haven't seen before and which are pivotal to task success, I would ensure the students see them at this stage, without necessarily making reference to the fact that it will come up in the listening task.

Pre-listening activities help to orient students' attention to the context and purpose of the upcoming task and can also prepare the way for further challenge either during or after the listening task takes place.

During pre-listening activities, I sometimes like to create spider diagrams with the students to explore word connections. This is because – like reading activities – if the students miss the pivotal word or phrase in a transcript, there will most likely be other cues which will lead them to the right response. For example, in the rather frustrating leisure activity exercise I referred to, a woman makes the pronouncement: "I go swimming in the swimming pool every morning at 6.30am. It is good for my health." If my students miss the actual activity, they should have acquired the necessary prior knowledge when learning about town buildings in order to use 'swimming pool' as a cue to getting the activity. As such, alerting students to the potential for secondary cues by exploring possible links and connections beforehand may be useful. At GCSE level, such pre-listening spider diagrams will also include synonyms, as quite often these are pivotal to successful task completion, particularly at higher-level GCSE. Of course, there is a balance to be found between preparing students effectively for listening activities and giving them too much 'guidance' in advance. However, in my experience, listening tends to be one of the skills which students are less motivated to undertake, and therefore optimising the potential for success while still implementing challenge can be worthwhile.

Often, particularly in the early years of language learning, we may require students to extrapolate one specific piece of information from listening – a day, a time, a place and so on. In the example of leisure activities, it may be the sport or activity we wish them to selectively hear. However, quite often listenings can be a mine of further golden opportunities which are left unexplored due to time pressures or a fear of prolonging what students may consider to be a 'boring' activity. In the swimming example on page 108, not only was a leisure activity mentioned but also a place, time and opinion. The potential for giving students further deliberate practice at finding pertinent information may merit re-listening to the transcript on a number of occasions.

Another example of implementing challenge may involve moving from a global understanding to a detailed under-standing, particularly for 'blind' listenings (e.g. listenings in preparation for GCSE exams when students will not know in advance what the context will be). If, for example, the transcript relates to a person's views on smoking, teachers may ask students through an initial listening to try to determine what the context is and whether they deem the person's views to be positive or negative. This first listening is also useful for giving students practice in picking up cues – they may perhaps write some notes to support their findings. These cues may include cognates they have heard or even voice inflection and intonation. On the second hearing, now that they are used to the pace and context, they could be given a detailed activity which assesses their acute understanding of the text. Such activities may include:

♦ Questions and answers in the target language or English.

♦ True/false questions.

♦ Multiple choice.

♦ Choosing the correct word to fill the gap.

Should it become clear that a number of students are not hearing the key information, replay the audio and pause it at the appropriate point to ensure that they do. After all, we would correct their verbal utterances and orient their attention to key information when evaluating a reading passage, so listenings should be no different.

As a post-listening activity, consider giving out the transcript and using it as a model to enhance the students' own outputs.

Speaking

While there is some evidence to suggest that students may generally enjoy speaking activities,[12] it is also the skill which can make them most anxious. As a former marker of speaking exams for an exam board, I have listened to recordings of students sobbing either before or partly through their exam. These were always very sensitively handled by the

---

12 See Gary Chambers, *Motivating Language Learners* (Clevedon: Multilingual Matters, 1999).

teachers, and typically the students went on to do quite well once they got over the trauma of the situation in which they found themselves!

I am reminded of a quote from a child called Andrew which appeared in a section of the Nuffield Foundation's report on *Languages* entitled 'Voices from the Classroom': "I don't like learning languages but I enjoy speaking them. I think this is because I can't get to grips with the hard learning of verbs, etc. Being in among a crowd of foreigners would help and therefore I could catch on and speak it in my own time."[13]

Ideally, in relation to speaking in the target language, we should seek an ethos which fosters high participation but low anxiety.[14] This can best be achieved through a classroom culture which places an emphasis on effective communication in speaking tasks in the early stages of language learning, as opposed to high-stakes accuracy of forms and structures (which is what I think Andrew is unknowingly saying), a culture which encourages students to take risks in their utterances, a culture which ensures that errors are viewed as part of the learning and are addressed sensitively, and a culture which challenges students to ask and respond to as many genuine open-ended questions as possible, thus offering opportunities to lengthen responses with meaningful and relevant information.

Maximising participation can also be a challenge in speaking. I am a fan of students reading aloud in the MFL classroom. I am also a fan of choral repetition and whole-class rehearsal. These definitely have their place, but obviously have limited scope for offering students the chance to manipulate language. Ideally, much speaking in the

---

13 Nuffield Foundation, *Languages: The Next Generation. The Final Report and Recommendations of the Nuffield Languages Enquiry* (2000), p. 47. Available at: https://www.nuffieldfoundation.org/sites/default/files/languages_finalreport.pdf.
14 See Suzanne Graham, Developing Speaking Skills in a Foreign Language. In Norbert Pachler and Ana Redondo (eds), *A Practical Guide to Teaching Foreign Languages in the Secondary School*, 2nd edn (Abingdon: Routledge, 2014), pp. 58–66.

classroom should be based around a certain purpose, such as the need to find out a piece of information from an interlocutor, which is crucial for successful task completion. In a Key Stage 3 class, this could be asking a peer in the target language for information and opinions on a matter in order to complete a class survey, such as what their favourite animal is or what pets they may have. In my experience, participation is maximised when students work in pairs as opposed to larger groups. In big groupings, some students may shy away and allow others to undertake the lion's share of the work. Moreover, purposeful pair work means that there is an obligation on both students to participate effectively in speaking tasks in order to plug the information gap before whole-class feedback on the task.

Further strategies for moving from whole-class oral work to pair work will be explored in Chapter 6.

Reading

Obviously, the use of reading texts can be highly beneficial in developing students' comprehension skills in the target language. Access to high-quality, accessible yet challenging texts for our learners, coupled with the effective deconstruction of the same texts through structured activities, should maximise the potential for modified output. This means that students should be able to manipulate the language they have seen in the text in order to enhance and embellish their own speaking and writing in the target language.

It is not the case that reading texts always have to be authentic – naturally, we may want to create new texts or tweak texts we have sourced in order to suit the ability of the students before us in the classroom. If we are honing in on a particular aspect of language structure or syntax, such as the present participle, we may wish to create a text which contains a number of different examples of the present participle.

Just like the other receptive skill of listening, reading in the target language is also most effective if we employ some pre-reading activities. These may include teaching specific vocabulary or grammatical items and brainstorming words and structures around a particular topic.

When students are provided with an extended text in the target language, it may be useful to 'break them in' with some warm-up activities. Typically this might include:

- Asking them to underline words they know in the target language.

- Asking them to identify any cognates in the text.

- Skimming and scanning for further clues as to the gist and tone of the text – for example, the use of negatives or the predominant tense used.

- Reading the text out loud. When read aloud by the teacher, the use of vocal inflection may assist students to grasp the initial tone of the text. When read aloud by the students themselves, it allows for further practice at phonetical accuracy.

Various activities can then be employed in order to dig deeper into the comprehension of the text. Such activities might include:

- True/false/not mentioned in the text.

- Multiple choice.

- Comprehension questions.

- Cloze exercises.

- Matching the start and end of sentences.

- Finish the sentence in free text.

- Find the synonyms.

- Translation.

Follow-up lessons might focus on how the text can be exploited for the purposes of modified output. This may include:

♦ Identifying key phrases for chunking in memory.

♦ Manipulating the text in order to talk or write about the students' own lives. For example, if the text is about healthy eating, they might adopt key language and structures to describe their own personal views about this topic.

♦ Presenting counterarguments. For example, if the text is about the advantages of social media, more advanced language learners may be tasked with presenting a counterargument article which outlines its dangers.

One concept worthy of note is that of 'narrow reading'. I first came across narrow reading in a post by Gianfranco Conti,[15] although the idea was proposed by Stephen Krashen.[16] This involves, for novice and even intermediate learners, reading several (possibly three to six) short passages on the same topic, with each passage containing very similar vocabulary and structures. This allows for significant exposure to structures and syntax while not appearing too repetitive.

An example of a narrow reading text may be as follows:

J'habite à Belfast en Irlande du Nord. C'est une grande ville industrielle qui se trouve au bord de la mer. Dans ma ville il y a la mairie, un port, plusieures usines, un centre de loisirs et des écoles. J'aime bien ma ville parce qu'il y a beaucoup de distractions; cependant il y a trop de pollution. (Claire)

15 Gianfranco Conti, Eight Narrow Reading Techniques That Will Enhance Your Students' Vocabulary and Reading Skills, *The Language Gym* [blog] (22 July 2017). Available at: https://gianfrancoconti.com/2017/07/22/eight-narrow-reading-techniques-that-will-enhance-your-students-vocabulary-and-reading-skills.

16 Stephen Krashen, The Case for Narrow Reading, *Language Magazine* 3(5) (2004): 17–19. Available at: http://www.sdkrashen.com/content/articles/2004_case_for_narrow_reading_lang_mag.pdf.

I live in Belfast in Northern Ireland. It is a big industrial town which is situated at the seaside. In my town there is a town hall, a port, several factories, a leisure centre and schools. I really like my town because there are lots of things to do; however, there is too much pollution. (Claire)

J'habite à Lisburn en Irlande du Nord. C'est une ville moyenne et touristique qui est située près de Belfast. Dans ma ville il y a la mairie, un centre commercial, plusieures usines, un centre de loisirs et des collèges. J'adore ma ville parce qu'il y a beaucoup de magasins; cependant il y a trop de voitures. (Paul)

I live in Lisburn in Northern Ireland. It is an average-sized tourist town which is situated near Belfast. In my town there is a town hall, a shopping centre, several factories, a leisure centre and secondary schools. I love my town because there are lots of shops; however, there are too many cars. (Paul)

J'habite à Lurgan en Irlande du Nord. C'est une petite ville industrielle qui se trouve à la campagne. Dans ma ville il y a l'hôtel de ville, une bibliothèque, plusieures usines, un centre de loisirs et un lycée. J'aime bien ma ville car il y a bon nombre de jardins publics; cependant il y a aussi trop de camions! (Ahmed)

I live in Lurgan in Northern Ireland. It is a small industrial town in the countryside. In my town there is a town hall, a library, several factories, a leisure centre and a school. I really like my town because there are plenty of parks; however, there are also too many lorries! (Ahmed)

In the same blog post, Gianfranco Conti suggests eight techniques for exploiting narrow reading texts:

1   Spot the differences – the students note down the differences in one text compared to two others.

2   Bad translation – the students are provided with three or four translated passages in which deliberate mistakes have been made. The students' task is to spot the mistakes, which encourages them to focus on vocabulary and sentence structures.

3   Summaries – students are given summaries of three to six passages and are asked to match the summary to the passage.

4   Pictures – the teacher selects a picture and creates three or more descriptions, only one of which is entirely accurate. The students must identify the right passage. This exercise is particularly useful for the GCSE photo card activity.

5   Questions – the students are provided with ten comprehension questions based on the three to six texts. Nine of the questions are answerable from the texts, but one is not. The students must identify the 'rogue' question.

6   Overgeneralisations – statements are produced which outline similarities in all the texts except one. For example, 'I live in the countryside' may apply to five of the six texts. The students must locate the text in which the statement does not appear.

7   Find the name – students put a name to the person to whom the sentence refers. For example: 'There are too many cars' links to Paul.

8   The most/the least – after creating a text, write some gapped sentences (e.g. 'The most musical person is …', 'The funniest person is …', 'The tallest person is …', 'The person who scored most goals is …') and the students fill in the gaps. Of course, this activity can also be linked in with the teaching of superlatives and comparatives.

Reflective Questions

◆ How do you build deliberate practice into lessons after teaching a skill?

◆ Are you giving students enough time to practise?

◆ Have you defined the knowledge you wish your students to practise?

◆ Have you built in opportunities for retrieval?

◆ What opportunities exist to maximise the potential of listening activities, including through pre-listening and post-listening tasks?

◆ Does the reading activity allow for a focus on structure and syntax?

Chapter 5

Feedback

In the previous lesson Rebekah spent a full hour writing an article for a school magazine in the target language as GCSE Higher Writing exam practice. The practice question asked her to outline in Spanish why her town was a good town and a memorable event she had attended in her locality. She wrote two full sides of A4 – much more than the required 150 words. However, quantity does not equate to quality, and her work is littered with errors. Accents are randomly distributed, she uses structures in the past after the time declension 'next weekend', sentence structures are incorrect and adjectival agreement is non-existent.

Her teacher, Mrs Monroe, spends two whole evenings marking the students' work and making comments. As well as marking and correcting the work in great detail for all twenty students, she writes two things that she really likes about their work and three targets.

Both Rebekah and Mrs Monroe have worked hard, but the feedback will prove ineffective. There is so much red pen and annotated correction on her work that Rebekah finds it difficult to see beyond it. She does not pick up on the corrected spellings and the omitted accents. Rebekah goes on to make similar and repeated errors in future assessments. The feedback has been largely ineffective.

The benefit of giving students good, timely feedback has a substantial weight of research evidence behind it. Providing feedback is one of the most effective and cost-effective ways of improving students' learning. In his study *Visible Learning: A Synthesis of 800 Meta-Analyses Relating to Achievement*, Hattie ranked 138 influences which have a bearing on learning outcomes – either positive or negative. The average effect size of all the interventions was 0.40. The updated effect sizes graph from 2018, however, shows feedback as having an effect size of 0.7 – considerably above the 0.4 threshold.[1]

We must be careful not to equate feedback to marking per se. Whole-school and departmental policies on feedback can focus almost entirely on marking. Feedback policies thus become marking policies, which place heightened and sometimes unrealistic demands on teachers' time and workload. We need to be wary of workload and what impact we want our feedback to have. On occasion, it may be the case that a different type of feedback is more appropriate and effective.

Additionally, feedback can be a double-edged sword. In the example of Rebekah, it may be the case that she cannot interpret the feedback in a manner which allows her to modify her linguistic output in a proactive manner. It is possibly also the case that time has not been afforded for her to reflect appropriately and effectively on the feedback given and targets suggested. If we get feedback wrong, we can damage student progress.

While the Education Endowment Foundation's research on marking indicates that the quality of existing evidence (focused specifically on written marking) is low, it also makes some recommendations. These include:

---

1 Sebastian Waack, Hattie Ranking: 252 Influences and Effect Sizes Related to Student Achievement, *Visible Learning* [blog] (2018). Available at: http://visible-learning.org/hattie-ranking-influences-effect-sizes-learning-achievement.

◊ *Careless mistakes should be marked differently to errors resulting from misunderstanding. The latter may be best addressed by providing hints or questions which lead pupils to underlying principles; the former by simply marking the mistake as incorrect, without giving the right answer*

◊ *Awarding grades for every piece of work may reduce the impact of marking, particularly if pupils become preoccupied with grades at the expense of a consideration of teachers' formative comments*

◊ *The use of targets to make marking as specific and actionable as possible is likely to increase pupil progress*

◊ *Pupils are unlikely to benefit from marking unless some time is set aside to enable pupils to consider and respond to marking*

◊ *Some forms of marking, including acknowledgement marking, are unlikely to enhance pupil progress. A mantra might be that schools should mark less in terms of the number of pieces of work marked, but mark better.*[2]

Not all marking in our classrooms is therefore ineffective. Sensible, precise and judicious marking has its place on a much bigger smorgasbord of feedback which will ensure that our students make maximum use of the feedback offered.

The strategies in this chapter aim to incorporate some of the recommendations from the Education Endowment Foundation's *A Marked Improvement?* However, the other feedback options on the smorgasbord go beyond the concept of traditional marking to include whole-class feedback, the

---

2   Victoria Elliott, Jo-Anne Baird, Therese Hopfenbeck, Jenni Ingram, Natalie Usher, Mae Zantout, Ian Thompson, James Richardson and Robbie Coleman, *A Marked Improvement? A Review of the Evidence on Written Marking* (London: Education Endowment Foundation, 2016), p. 5. Available at: https://educationendowmentfoundation.org.uk/public/files/Presentations/Publications/EEF_Marking_Review_April_2016.pdf.

use of prompt sheets and checklists, code systems for giving feedback and identifying targets, individual verbal feedback, live marking, highlighting, peer feedback and self-reflection. Each has its own principles to follow, and equally its own pitfalls, of which we must be aware. Having a strong understanding of the value of the feedback we already give and widening the array of feedback tools at our disposal can help us to keep workload in perspective without diminishing the impact of feedback.

Feedback has the following main roles: to show students what they need to aim for, to set them off and then to keep their learning on track, to let them know that they have got there and to point them in the direction of their next goal. Throughout this iterative journey, feedback will be at its best when it is a reciprocal process – an ongoing to-ing and fro-ing of information between teacher and student. It is not a one-way street.

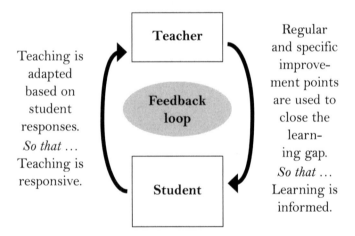

The information we receive back from students – through assessments, assignments, low-stakes testing, quizzing or their response to feedback – should ultimately inform our approach to teaching. Dylan Wiliam refers to this as 'responsive teaching'.[3] Such information allows us to identify learning gaps, misconceptions and potential embedded errors (as opposed to one-off mistakes), and it enables us to modify our teaching approach in the classroom accordingly – immediately if needs be – in order to address the issue. Feedback in this manner can inform our future teaching, thus completing the feedback loop.

Following the identification of a 'learning gap', feedback should be aimed at closing this gap. Imagine I have set a GCSE writing task on the environment, part of which requires the students to write about 'un mundo ideal' (an ideal world) from an environmental viewpoint. While circulating the room and observing their work, I note that some students are failing to address this point, and some who are attempting it are not using the conditional tense accurately. My gut instinct may be to remind students that they covered the conditional tense some months prior and to go back to their notes independently. However, no matter how students acquire grammatical rules – whether inductively, deductively or explicitly – they will frequently need to be re-exposed to pertinent forms and structures through modelling and guided practice. In this instance, I therefore view the conditional tense as a 'learning gap' and reteach it, explaining how they could develop their answer to include it. While doing this, I might also take a few moments to remind them of how we have used the conditional tense in previous contexts and topics, and when and how we are going to use it in the future:

We have just seen how we can incorporate the phrase 'no habría más atascos de tráfico' (there would be no more traffic jams) into our work. You may remember that we explored the phrase 'no habría más' in the context of an ideal school – 'no habría más uniforme escolar' (there would be no more school uniform) – and we will come

---

3   See https://twitter.com/dylanwiliam/status/393045049337847808.

across it again when we consider an ideal future – 'no habría más guerra' (there would not be any war).

In this way, I am hopefully not just giving feedback in a manner which is closing the learning gap, but essentially also 'feeding forward' by orienting students' attention to the fact that they will need to be able to transfer the conditional structures again in future months. Our feedback as teachers must be specific in relation to what exactly students need to do in order to improve their future learning and how to do it, rather than focusing on what is deficient in their work. Had I just given students the feedback to 'review the conditional tense', it is quite possible that minimal if any improvement may have been made in subsequent redrafts or future written work where the structures need to be transferred. In his book *Embedded Formative Assessment*, Dylan Wiliam tells the story of a science student who is given feedback to be 'more systematic' in planning his scientific enquiries. The student retorts that had he known how to be systematic, he would have done it the first time. Wiliam continues to compare such feedback to telling an unsuccessful comedian to be funnier – accurate but unhelpful.[4] As Wiliam points out in a later article on feedback: "If there's a single principle teachers need to digest about classroom feedback, it's this: *The only thing that matters is what students do with it.*"[5]

Feedback can inform our future planning at a micro-level – in lessons as we move swiftly to address any misconceptions or errors based on feedback, in-between lessons as we reflect and evaluate, and in-between units of work as we modify them based on responsive teaching approaches – and when reviewing the curriculum at a macro-level.

4   Dylan Wiliam, *Embedded Formative Assessment* (Bloomington, IN: Solution Tree Press, 2011), p. 120.
5   Dylan Wiliam, Is the Feedback You're Giving Students Helping or Hindering? *Dylan Wiliam Center* (29 November 2014) (original emphasis). Available at: https://www.dylanwiliamcenter.com/is-the-feedback-you-are-giving-students-helping-or-hindering.

The strategies in this chapter focus on three key areas: how to improve the quality of in-the-moment feedback, how to improve the efficacy and quality of marking, and how to improve approaches to peer and self-checking.

1. Mini Whiteboards

In Chapters 1 and 4 we discussed the importance of retrieval practice for embedding linguistic knowledge in long-term memory. I find mini whiteboards really useful for this purpose in the MFL classroom. They are also a highly beneficial tool for teachers because they give us instant feedback about how well the class know or have understood an aspect of the language. I have found them to be an absolutely invaluable addition to my classroom. As an example, I might ask students to conjugate a verb from an infinitive and pronoun which are on the screen. Sometimes I might offer them a multiple choice of possible conjugations. Such an activity works well on the mini whiteboards because the answer is either right or wrong. Experience has taught me that students typically manage well when asked to conjugate with a pronoun, but may struggle when proper nouns are used. They may be able to conjugate:

yo (vivir) _____

But will struggle with

Señor y Señora Gómez (vivir) _____

In acknowledgement of this potential learning gap, I might ask the students to write out the conjugated verb for the pronoun question, but give them a multiple choice for the question with a proper noun. This allows me to discuss with the class in some detail why three of the four choices are not appropriate and why the correct answer is, potentially also giving examples of proper nouns which could be used with the three wrong choices, thus hopefully reinforcing knowledge:

Señor y Señora Gómez _____

1 *vivo*

2 *vive*

3 *vivimos*

4 *viven*

There are some simple but effective strategies which can be employed to get the most out of mini whiteboards.

♦ Having given the students a question, allocate a certain amount of time for them to write their answers before getting them to raise their boards at the same time. If they are allowed to raise the boards as soon as they have completed the answer, there is the risk that some students may choose to copy down the answer from someone whose board was raised quickly! Counting down from three and then getting them to show resolves this (*Drei, zwei, eins, los!*).

♦ Interrogate students on their answers (e.g. Why did you choose that answer? Where do you think you went wrong with that answer?). If there is an error, such as a missing accent, pick up on this (e.g. Can you think of something that might be missing from your answer, John?). Or ask another student if they can identify a mistake in someone else's response and correct it.

♦ If numerous students are getting the answer wrong, use this feedback responsively by reteaching the element in question.

♦ Space it out. If you are using mini whiteboards for the purpose of retrieval practice to test students' knowledge of prior lessons, throw in questions which ask them to retrieve information from a few weeks ago, last month, a term ago or even previous years. This will not only strengthen the knowledge in long-term memory, but will also be useful feedback about what gaps or misconceptions may still be there.

2. Get in Early

Research indicates that the earlier a mistake is corrected while learning something new, the faster the information will be learnt, as you can't labour effectively under a misconception.[6] When asking closed questions in the classroom, it is of course easy to give immediate feedback – as we can see from the prior example of using mini whiteboards. It is possible to give early feedback in a range of contexts in the MFL classroom. Indeed, the *Modern Foreign Languages Pedagogy Review* views this as essential: "Error correction in both spoken and written language is most powerful when it can be done immediately."[7]

---

6   James A. Kulik and Chen-Lin C. Kulik, Timing of Feedback and Verbal Learning, *Review of Educational Research*, 58(1) (1988): 79–97.
7   Bauckham, *Modern Foreign Languages Pedagogy Review*, p. 15.

Say it

Whereas written feedback can be time-consuming, verbal feedback is quick, simple and in-the-moment. At my own school, we don't accept it when students make grammatical mistakes in English. A student who says 'I done' or 'the bell has went' is immediately corrected. We apply the same approach in the MFL classroom to spoken language, albeit (hopefully) in a warm and supportive manner. Some people may worry that an immediate response to pronunciation and grammar correction in the MFL classroom may inhibit students and make them more reluctant to communicate orally. I have not found this to be the case. Typically, student utterances at a whole-class level are limited to, at most, a few sentences in any given lesson, meaning that they are not being bombarded with numerous corrections. It is also possible to inject a little humour into the correction phase, which often helps. For example, I frequently find myself having to correct students' pronunciation of '-tion' endings in French, such as 'la natation'. Typically, a student will pronounce it with a loose 'sh' instead of a very sharp 'ss'. When correcting, I sometimes really over-exaggerate the accurate sound, which the students then endeavour to replicate in an equally overemphasised manner. It quite often engenders a laugh and removes any feelings of self-consciousness.

While robust and immediate error correction in spoken language is beneficial and effective, it is perhaps worth noting that there may be times when we wish to seek a balance between fluency and accuracy. This is particularly the case if students are given a very extended response in the classroom. For example, if they are reading aloud a paragraph they have written for homework in the target language, it might be counterproductive for me to pick up on and correct every single mistake, as this will evidently break the flow and slow things down, but it may also be detrimental to the student's confidence in speaking in the target language. On this occasion, it may be more judicious to identify a select number of mistakes for correction once she has finished.

Quite often whole-class drill and rehearsal allows for feedback on spoken language. The use of knowledge organisers has led to many of my lessons beginning with a rehearsal of PROFS sentences (as discussed in Chapter 2). As students enter the room, I will be saying phrases in English which they are required to recite back in French. This allows for me to hone in with the class on any awry pronunciation and practise it specifically.

Much target language interaction in the classroom is undertaken in pairs to enhance the amount of time students get to practise their language. This can have the added benefit of ensuring that the verbal feedback we give to a student as we circulate is more personal, especially if the student is daunted by having to correct mistakes in a large group setting.

Of course, verbal feedback is not just limited to oral work. As we move around the classroom when students are undertaking written practice activities, verbal feedback could focus on a number of aspects, including:

◆ To encourage students to think about high-level vocabulary in terms of content.

◆ To draw attention to inaccuracies in spelling or grammar.

◆ To develop thinking about high-quality functional use of language, such as extended justification of opinions.

◆ To induce thinking on the structure of responses.

Once we have given feedback, there should always be an expectation that students do something about it. For example, if a student has made a minor mistake in spelling and you have drawn their attention to it, you may want them to have a go at spelling it out for you accurately. If the spelling mistake is more acute and you suspect it is due to a slapdash approach or failure to check their vocabulary book or notes, as is good practice, you may want to advise them of the mistake and that you will be back in a moment or two to verify that the student has corrected it by consulting their notes properly. If your verbal feedback contains a number of pointers for improvement of work, it might be an idea to ask the student to repeat back to you the feedback you have given in their own words or to ask them, "What is the first thing you intend to do?"

Seating plans

When using mini whiteboards to test students' understanding of verb conjugations, it is possible to see quickly who hasn't grasped the process of conjugation. As a result, I can tweak my seating plan to make sure that those who need additional support and 'check-ins' are placed strategically so that they are in easy reach and grouped in a manner which allows me to work with them in pairs or threes. Reviewing seating plans as and when necessary ensures that the students who need the most input are easily accessible.

Walk with a pen or highlighter

Experience allows us to decide with professional discretion the level of feedback we feel we need to give a student in the classroom. As we observe a student's work, it may become evident that errors are being made which expose a lack of understanding of an underlying principle. At this point, in line with the Education Endowment Foundation recommendations referred to earlier in this chapter, we may wish to spend time with the student addressing this gap through feedback; or if it is an error being made by numerous students, it may be more prudent to address it within a larger group or whole-class setting. These are what the Education

Endowment Foundation refer to in *A Marked Improvement?* as 'errors' in their distinction between 'errors' and 'mistakes'.

If it is a 'mistake' which you know a student has the capability of correcting for themselves independently, then perhaps it may be more beneficial to draw their attention to it as you move around the classroom and request that they rectify it. Whether they have spelt a word incorrectly, conjugated erroneously, mixed up the word order or even used a cognate when a more high-level word would have been more appropriate, using a highlighter or pen on their work to draw it to their attention is a possible feedback strategy. Often, you can tell the student that you will return in a few minutes to ensure that the mistake has been corrected. This ensures self-reflection on the part of the student. Additionally, if you highlight a word without any accompanying discourse with the student, they have to think for themselves about the nature of the mistake: have I spelt the word incorrectly? Is the ending wrong? Does the word make sense within the context? Should I have used a different word?

On occasion, you may wish to advise students in advance what you will be looking out for in terms of feedback through highlighting. For example, you might say, "While I will be highlighting any general mistakes in red pen, I will be specifically highlighting any misuse or inaccuracies in the pluperfect tense with a blue highlighter." This is particularly useful after an aspect of language has just been taught or if you wish to revisit a particular element of linguistic use.

As we will see later in this chapter, it is possible that you will also have codes for marking, such as 'O+J' to indicate the need for the development of opinions and justification in a piece of work. Of course, these codes can also be deployed when a student is undertaking the work, as a means of 'getting in early' with feedback rather than waiting until the work is finished and handed in.

Spotlight an example

As discussed in Chapter 3, if you find an example among student work worthy of merit and praise, read it aloud or put it under the visualiser. Solicit responses from the class about why it is so good and how it could be developed further. Remember to praise the student in question for their excellent use of language in front of the whole class. Social norms are important.

Stop the bus

Sometimes the information we receive back from our students in terms of linguistic output will suggest to us that the most effective form of feedback we can give is to press the emergency stop button and reteach an element of language, especially if many students are getting it wrong. If this happens, we should not underestimate the importance of this 'responsive teaching', and should not concern ourselves unduly that it may slow down the coverage of curriculum content. In the long run, my experience suggests to me that time spent in this manner is time well spent. Students' language skills become better embedded through the reconsolidation of linguistic knowledge, thus creating a better foundation on which their skills can be built and extended.

3. Checklists

Checklists can be a useful tool in assisting students with the process of reviewing and editing their work prior to handing it in. Reviewing and editing are not strategies which come easily to students. No doubt you will have come across students whose primary goal with written work is task completion, who rush through it at breakneck speed so they can put their pen down and slouch back in their chair convinced in the knowledge that they have done what has been asked of them. Even in exam situations, I often find myself explicitly having to prompt students who are sitting with the paper closed before them to review and check their work, no matter what the subject.

In order to support students with reviewing and editing their work, and also to minimise the potential for careless mistakes, we could consider giving them a checklist like the one below which can be used to check their work as they go. Checklists can be modified, of course, to suit the specific purpose and focus of tasks.

Have you ...	Tick
Used appropriate vocabulary to communicate clearly?	
Used a broad range of vocabulary to avoid repetition and minimise cognates?	
Checked the spelling of high-level and high-frequency words?	
Included adjectives, adverbs and quantifiers to enrich description?	
Checked adjective endings for accuracy?	
Included a range of tenses, including present, past, future and conditional?	
Checked the accuracy of auxiliary verbs?	

Have you …	Tick
Checked verb conjugations?	
Included opinions?	
Ensured that opinions are justified as much as possible?	
Reviewed word order?	

When checklists are comprised of clear statements, perhaps aligned to mark schemes, students can easily interpret them and check their work accordingly. Like all scaffolds, we may want to gradually remove them as our students progress on their journey from beginner in the language to fluency, from dependent to independent.

4. Mark Smart

When work is handed in for marking, experienced MFL teachers have an array of strategies for ensuring that marking is manageable, while also making sure that feedback is effective and that the lion's share of responsibility for reviewing and editing is placed on the student.

Use codes	Create a list of common codes, for example: VT – verb tenses, VC – verb conjugation, WO – word order, AA – adjectival agreement, SP – spelling. By pre-empting the code with an 'S' for success or a 'T' for target, you can identify for the student whether the code refers to something they are being praised for or whether their work indicates that it is a target for development. For example, T–VT would indicate that the student needs to work on the accuracy of their tense usage. You could define this even further by giving each tense a number. T–VT2 might indicate that specific inaccuracies are noticeable in the past tense. S–VT3 would indicate that the student has used the future tense effectively. You can, of course, temper the codes with short comments, for example, "¡Muy bien, Jacob! S–AA." If you are using codes as a target, you will most likely need to explain to students how they can be actioned to bring about improvement. Telling a student that they need to improve the accuracy of their tense usage will not miraculously bring about this improvement. Further strategies in this table, such as 'collating errors' and 'using examples as feedback', will give some opportunities for responsive teaching in this regard.

Use tick-lists	Print out your list of successes and targets as a tick-list. Mark those that apply for the student. This tick-list could be aligned to the checklist discussed in section 3 of this chapter.
Circle 'mistakes'	If a student has made a mistake which you expect them to be able to fix independently without explicit feedback, such as a careless spelling mistake, simply circle or underline it.
Collate 'errors'	When marking, you might wish to keep a separate sheet beside you on which you note common errors as they are occurring in students' work. Rather than writing the same feedback on 20 individual pieces of student work, it may be more prudent, and a better use of time, to address these errors in a whole-class feedback session. This has the added benefit of giving you an additional degree of control in relation to the interpretation of the feedback. Feedback succeeds or fails depending on what students do with it. Delivering whole-class feedback, especially in response to common errors, allows you greater opportunity to ensure it is properly understood and acted upon.

Use peers	Peer marking can be a fraught and dangerous process; however, a checklist or tick-list can help to scaffold and structure the marking process. To mitigate against the possibility that peers may not mark accurately, you can check it and either write that you agree with it or overrule any inaccuracies.
Return it quickly	Feedback is probably most effective and most appreciated by students when it is given in a timely manner. This can be even more effective than writing lots of extra detail and it taking longer as a result.
Examples as feedback	Another strategy which can be employed as a substitute to writing extended comments is to show the class examples of the best work produced. This can often avoid the abstract language in which some marking rubrics are written.

5. Expect a Response

Students are unlikely to benefit from our feedback unless we set aside time for them to reflect on it, review strategies to meet targets and action improvement. As a result, it is incumbent upon us to allocate time for them to do this. This runs contrary to the misguided belief that we should be pushing on at all times with curriculum content, and therefore that time is not available for student reflection. On the contrary, dedicated improvement and reflection time (DIRT) can be a key element in ensuring that students become perfect in their practice and in expediting their journey to independence and fluency in language use. Whether it is a question of a few minutes to reflect on performance following a low-stakes retrieval quiz or a 'pause' lesson in order to reflect extensively on feedback, DIRT is an essential component of effective feedback. In sporting terms, it can be the equivalent of a 100-metre sprinter pausing to review a video of her performance and analysing her technique in intricate detail, setting targets for future improvement accordingly.

DIRT is usually most effective if we give students time to correct any mistakes we may have circled or coded. It is good practice for them to use a different coloured pen when doing so, as it reinforces their own accountability. Some teachers ask their students to put right their spelling mistakes a number of times in the hope that it reinforces accuracy. It is also sound practice if they endeavour to seek out and rectify mistakes independently in the first instance, as this is an important skill. At an appropriate time, you may wish to give students the opportunity to seek further assistance from yourself or a peer.

While the nature of feedback is very often context-specific, not least in relation to how well the class have completed the task, some further strategies for DIRT may include:

♦ Show and discuss a good model answer from a student in the class and have the remaining students edit their own responses as a result.

♦ Undertake a live model with the class, during which you co-construct an excellent response. This live model could focus to a large extent on the rectification of mistakes made by students in their original work.

♦ Provide students with writing frames or scaffolds based on specific target codes which allow them to rewrite all or part of their work.

♦ Request that students redraft the entire piece.

♦ Provide students with the opportunity to translate the feedback into a different context, which affords them an opportunity to meet targets. For example, if you have advised them that they need to target accuracy in their use of adjectives, and the original piece of work was based on relationships with family members, ask the students to complete a piece in which they describe their best friend and expound on the characteristics of an ideal friend or future partner.

Reflecting on and redrafting written work is an important strategy as we strive for fluency in a language. However, as MFL teachers we must ensure that our students have ample opportunity to practise in an increasingly independent manner. After all, a perfectly redrafted piece of work stuck into a classwork book is no indication of capability. Only when a high standard of work can be repeated independently can we be confident that real learning has taken place.

6. Feedback on Speaking

A large part of preparing our students for speaking assessments and examinations is in ensuring that their written responses to speaking questions are detailed and accurate, communicating a clear answer to the question posed. In this regard, approaches to feedback discussed already in this chapter will be pertinent as we prepare them for speaking examinations.

When it comes to feedback on pronunciation, this can be a challenge in MFL classes with a large number of students. The following chapter on questioning will explore some strategies for this within MFL lessons. However, some MFL teachers mark spoken assessments and provide individualised phonics support using virtual classroom software, assignment and feedback apps such as Showbie (www.showbie.com) and self-quizzing sites like Quizlet.

Reflective Questions

Our feedback should not discourage students from tackling difficulties, meeting challenge head-on or taking risks. Feedback may look very different depending on the context, and therefore we should have a battery of different feedback styles that are familiar to our students so they can access them effectively. Feedback should be timely and relevant. We must also make dedicated time for students to respond to our feedback by redrafting their work or following up on our suggestions in terms of grammar and pronunciation practice.

♦ Does your feedback help you and your students know whether or not they are secure with the key knowledge?

♦ Does your feedback encourage the students to think about how they could improve their work?

♦ Do you ensure that the students respond to the feedback you give them?

♦ Is the feedback you use manageable and sustainable?

♦ Do you use feedback to help you inform your planning?

♦ If you use peer or self-feedback, how do you ensure that it doesn't compound misconceptions?

Chapter 6

Questioning

Mr Maxwell is teaching noun gender in Spanish to his Year 7 class using the topic of 'classroom items'. He spends a good part of the lesson laboriously emphasising the distinction between 'el' and 'la' as he holds up various objects (e.g. 'el borrador', 'la carpeta') – without telling the students upfront why he is doing this. Then comes the crux of the lesson, when he asks the students why he is making the above distinctions in his verbal utterances, which are now displayed in written format in all their glory on the interactive whiteboard. Silence. After some awkward, fumbling questioning on Mr Maxwell's part, the class finally 'discover' the notion of noun gender and that Spanish nouns typically are either masculine or feminine. Mr Maxwell then takes it a step further by pointing the students to the noun 'las tijeras' (scissors) and asking them to work out why it starts with 'las' and not 'el' or 'la' (hoping they will deduce that scissors are plural). One hand goes up at the back of the room. "Sir," comes the reply in all innocence, "is that the transgender one?"

Even after almost twenty years in the classroom, MFL teaching never ceases to surprise, amuse and amaze me. It is what makes it, quite simply, the best job ever. I have used my own name in the above example – it is a true story from my own classroom. Looking back, I can now see how futile my approach was. The concept of noun gender is somewhat alien to English-speaking students who do not have the background knowledge that most Indo-European languages have noun gender – some languages, like German, even have a neuter as well as a masculine and feminine. The ultimate answer given by the student was a comical reflection of societal change, but an even bigger reflection on the failure of my questioning techniques. The students simply did not have the cultural knowledge in order to answer my questions. I was playing a game with them of 'guess what's in the teacher's head'. If I were to do the lesson again, I would probably just teach the students the knowledge and give them plenty of deliberate practice. If anything, this interaction reinforced for me the importance of planning questions a little in advance, and ensuring that they enable the students to demonstrate and extend their existing knowledge.

All subject domains in the curriculum, without exception, rely on questioning. MFL is no different. Just as questioning will pervade most lessons in a school on a given day, so too will it play a prominent role in MFL lessons – whether in the target or first language. Indeed, Rosenshine concludes that effective teachers ask significantly more questions than less effective teachers.[1] For our MFL students to become fluent, they must develop the ability to ask relevant questions and answer appropriately in the target language. The opportunities that we as teachers give them to ask and answer questions in the target language, coupled with the questions we ask them in the first language in order to underpin their linguistic knowledge, can have a significant bearing on the pace of their journey from beginner to expert.

---

1 Rosenshine, Principles of Instruction, p. 14.

As teachers of MFL, now is perhaps an opportune moment to stop and think about why we ask our students questions:

- To encourage them to retrieve information from memory in order to strengthen it.

- To highlight links to prior learning.

- To test understanding of a linguistic concept.

- To offer opportunities for linguistic output.

- To develop and deepen understanding of a linguistic concept.

- To encourage a focus on the semantics and phonics of language, and to foster an understanding of similarities and differences between their first language and the target language.

- To give them opportunities to respond in the target language to unprepared situations.

In many ways, the notion of questioning to improve recall, check understanding and deepen thinking rings true no matter what the subject. Therefore, as in all subjects, it is important that we establish culture, routine and expectations with regard to questioning early on in a student's language learning experience. This involves: ensuring that the answering of questions is shared as widely as possible around the class in a given lesson; using questions as a mechanism to guarantee that all students are participating in the cognitive work of the lesson; encouraging them to take risks with their responses and to view mistakes as an opportunity to grow their relevant knowledge and skills; and making students feel comfortable about asking questions themselves.

Yet we must also be conscious of the fact that MFL teaching is a very different animal to other disciplines. Deep, probing questioning in the history classroom with the purpose of eliciting advanced, analytical responses from students is unlike the potential purpose of questioning in the MFL classroom, not least because the students are often expected to respond in a language which isn't their native one. Language teacher Steve Smith puts it like this: "Language teaching is not like the teaching of, say, mathematics or history. Much of our questioning is of a special type, with the purpose of developing internalised competence with grammar, vocabulary and, ultimately, fluency."[2]

As well as making students feel at ease about asking subject-related questions, we must also ensure that we create a culture in which students feel comfortable answering them. Again, this is where MFL teaching perhaps differs from teaching in other subjects. There is no doubt that some students may feel more reticent when answering questions orally in the MFL classroom, particularly if it is in the target language, due to a lack of knowledge, embarrassment or a feeling, sadly, that it is 'uncool'.

There are strategies which can be employed from early on in a student's language learning experience which will help to mitigate against embarrassment and reticence, including reading aloud and a focus on phonics when practising speaking. Later on in this chapter, we will look at some more practical strategies. If the barrier to answering a question stems from a gap in a student's knowledge, quite often our strategy is to move on quickly to a different student and try to elicit the answer from them. The difficulty with this is that it, in turn, may lead to the original student experiencing the embarrassment of not knowing the answer and of a peer being called on to dig him out of a hole. There may sometimes be a good reason for moving on to another student in this manner; after all, there is no point in flogging a dead horse. However, a better strategy perhaps may be to help the original student get to the right answer through questions which prompt him towards the solution:

---

2   Steve Smith, Pace, Challenge and Questions, *Language Teacher Toolkit* [blog] (25 July 2012). Available at: http://frenchteachernet.blogspot.co.uk/2012/07/pace-challenge-and-questions.html.

Teacher: Can you tell me what 'à pied' means, John?

John: I don't know.

Teacher: OK. Do you remember when we saw it some weeks ago, we compared it with an English word which commenced with 'ped'. Do you remember what that word was?

John: Was it 'pedestrian'?

Teacher: That's right, John. What is a pedestrian?

John: Someone who is walking to get to a place.

Teacher: So what do you think 'à pied' might mean?

John: By foot.

Another strategy to avoid reticence or gaps in students' knowledge may be to employ think-pair-share time before asking for a response. If students have the opportunity to bounce a response off a peer before delivering it in front of the whole class, this has the potential not only to give them a little more confidence but also to heighten the accuracy of their response. This strategy can be employed when asking students to verbalise structures as deliberate practice. For example, if I had just taught the future in Spanish using the verb 'ir' + 'a' + infinitive, a typical questioning session might go like this:

Teacher: Remind me of the structuring of future sentences we have been looking at. What comes first (pause) ... James?

James: Conjugation of the verb 'ir' followed by 'a'.

Teacher: Well done, James. What comes next (pause) ... Céline?

Céline: The infinitive.

Teacher: Well done, Céline. Infinitives in Spanish end in one of three ways. What are they (pause) … Mark?

Mark: -ar, -ir and -er.

Teacher: Good, Mark. What finishes our sentence (pause) … Rafal?

Rafal: An 'added extra'.

Teacher: Can you elaborate on that, Rafal?

Rafal: Well, if we were saying we were going to travel somewhere, the added extra might be where we are going to travel to or how we are going to travel there.

Teacher: Excellent. Can you remind me of what else enriches our future statements (pause) … Goncalo?

Goncalo: Putting in when you are going to do it, like next weekend or next year.

Teacher: ¡*Formidable!* You all now have twenty seconds with your partner to tease out how you would say, "Tomorrow I am going to download music onto my phone."

The rest of this chapter will focus on strategies that can be employed in the MFL classroom in order to develop our students' ability to ask and answer questions effectively in the target language, as well as maximising the effect of the questions we ask as teachers in order to ensure the solidity of the underpinning linguistic knowledge.

1. Directed Questioning

Put simply, directed questioning is when the teacher chooses who answers the question without the aid of a hands-up rule or random approach, such as using an online name generator. By directing questions a teacher can create a culture in which every student expects to be asked a question, thus by default raising the challenge level for all. It is this approach, more than any other, which in my opinion makes best use of a teacher's professional judgement and discretion when questioning. Through the planning of questions beforehand or 'gut instinct' on the spur of the moment in the classroom, which comes from experience and knowing the class well, directed questioning allows teachers to tailor the questions asked. Directed questioning also affords the teacher opportunities to give that low-ability student a confidence boost by asking them a question which will allow them to demonstrate their knowledge. Teachers can make determinations on which students should be pushed and challenged through directed questioning on specific contexts as well as which questions may need to be directed at particular students in order to eradicate misconceptions.

You may have noted that in the examples in the prior section, the teacher asked the question before selecting a student. Instead of saying: "Billy, welche Unterschiede gibt es zwischen deutschen und britischen Schulen?" (Billy, what differences are there between German and British schools?), it is preferable to reshape the question like this: "Welche Unterschiede gibt es zwischen deutschen und britischen Schulen … Billy?" If we put the name of the student to be asked at the start of the question it has the potential to let all the other students off the hook or even to drift off for a moment or two. By asking the question before saying the name – preferably with a pause before the name – all students are obliged to think about a possible response because, following the pause, they could be the one asked.

Of course, we can employ other strategies in our endeavour to involve everyone in the questioning process: in Chapter 5 we discussed the use of mini whiteboards, while the use of apps such as Quizlet, Quizlet Live, Kahoot and even Google Classroom enable us to set quizzes and collate student responses. Used well, they can also advise us of what gaps in knowledge individual students are manifesting and potential interventions for eradicating those gaps.

2. Questioning for Prior Learning

In the anecdote at the beginning of this chapter, the mistake that I undoubtedly made was to question students on something of which they had no prior knowledge. This notion of 'guess what's in the teacher's head' is foolish. However, given the cumulative aspect of language learning there should be many opportunities to question for prior learning. As an example, we have already discussed retrieval practice extensively in Chapters 1 and 4. In Chapter 1, we also explored how potential contexts for learning may evolve and deepen over time. For example, in Year 7, knowledge about family members and pets may evolve and deepen until, by Year 10, the students are exploring marriage and relationships in the target language.

Before starting a new context at GCSE level, it may be worthwhile to question students on their prior knowledge under a number of subheadings. Often this may take the form of a template page on which students complete different columns in a think-pair-share activity.

Let's take the topic of 'food and eating out' as an example.

♦ Vocabulary (food and drink vocabulary).

- Adjectives for justification (delicious, disgusting, juicy, salty, tasty, etc.).

- Typical and high-frequency verbs.

- Chunked phrases (e.g. I would like to order, Do you have …?).

3. Reinforce Question Words Early

When I reflect on my early teaching, the frequency of specific target language questions such as "What is … in German?" and "How do you spell that?" meant that my students often became very familiar with such questions because I was asking them so frequently. In the 'good old days' of overhead projectors, I would often teach vocabulary through pictures that I would cut out of acetate paper. I would then turn the overhead projector off, take a picture away and ask the question, "What is missing?" My students would be very familiar with this question as well.

Ironically, however, I invariably failed to teach students the high-frequency question words which form such an inextricable part of communication. While my students knew specific questions relevant to classroom activities, it was only in Year 9 that they were explicitly taught question words:

- What …?

- Where …?

- When …?

- How …?

- Why …?

- How much …?

- Which …?

Nowadays, I teach these words at a very early stage in Year 7 and use every opportunity to implement them in classroom activities. For example, while teaching prepositions in the context of 'house and home' in Year 7, I would present images and ask:

♦ Where are the books?

♦ How many books are there?

♦ Which book is on the table?

♦ What is under the bed?

Taking time to link question words to types of response is also worthwhile. For example, when asking a question in the target language which uses the form 'how many', I would take a moment at an appropriate juncture in the process to remind students that 'how many' will require a number in the response. Similarly, 'when' will require a time phrase in the target language, such as a day or date, and 'why' will require a reason, often using 'because'. It is advantageous to embed and reinforce these links with students.

With the return in revised GCSE specifications to role play scenarios and even photo cards with some exam boards – including the need for students to ask questions and respond to unpredictable questions – the importance of incorporating high-frequency question words in the target language into lessons at every opportunity is clear. The earlier we do this, the better.

It is possible to design activities which require the students to formulate questions. For example, while studying 'extreme sports' in Year 10, the students might be presented with a series of answers and asked in pairs to consider what a likely question may have been:

♦ Answer: *Deux fois.* (Two times.)

Possible question: *Combien de fois as-tu fait de la plongée sous-marine?* (How many times have you done deep-sea diving?)

♦ Answer: *Je voulais découvrir quelque chose de nouveau et d'in-habituel.* (I wanted to try something new and unusual.)

Possible question: *Pourquoi est-ce que tu fais de la plongée sous-marine?* (Why do you do deep-sea diving?)

♦ Answer: *Je fais cette activité sportive depuis l'âge de douze ans.* (I've been doing this sporting activity since the age of 12).

Possible question: *Depuis quand est-ce que tu fais de la plongée sous-marine?* (Since when have you been doing deep-sea diving?)

4. The Teacher–Student Practice Method

In Chapter 3, we explored the significance of drill and rehearsal for developing students' pronunciation when speaking. As a beginning teacher, one method I learnt which has stood the test of time, and which I still use regularly in order to develop students' practice in moving orally from single words to extended answers involving the formulation of questions, is what I call teacher–student practice. This is detailed in Wendy Phipps' *Pairwork*, which is part of the CILT Pathfinders Series.[3] If T stands for teacher and S for student, the steps would look something like this:

Step 1: T–S

The teacher asks a question to individual students:

T: *Gefällt dir Deutsch?* (Do you like German?)

---

3   Wendy Phipps, *Pairwork: Interaction in the Modern Languages Classroom* (Pathfinder Series) (London: CILT, 1999).

S1: *Ja.* (Yes.)

T: *Gefällt dir Geschichte?* (Do you like history?)

S2: *Nein.* (No.)

Step 2: S–T

The teacher then asks students to pose a series of questions to him or her:

S1: *Gefällt Ihnen Mathe?* (Do you like maths?)

T: *Nein, Mathe gefällt mir nicht.* (No, I don't like maths.)

S2: *Gefällt Ihnen Erdkunde?* (Do you like geography?)

T: *Ja, Erdkunde gefällt mir.* (Yes, I like geography.)

Note that the teacher is now modelling full sentences.

Step 3: S–S

The teacher then facilitates 'open pair' practice, in which a student in one part of the classroom poses a question to a student in another part of the room:

S1: *Gefällt dir Englisch?* (Do you like English?)

S2: *Ja, Englisch gefällt mir.* (Yes, I like English.)

S3: *Gefällt dir Latein?* (Do you like Latin?)

S4: *Nein, Latein gefällt mir nicht.* (No, I don't like Latin.)

This can then be followed by pair work with the person beside them. In this manner, the students know what is required and expected of them.

Depending on the context of the learning, the teacher–student cycle can be repeated either partially or in its entirety to extend answers and provide justifications. At this stage, it may be useful for the students to have a scaffold crib sheet in order to support their statements:

Step 2: S–T

S: *Gefällt Ihnen Kunst?* (Do you like art?)

T: *Nein, Kunst gefällt mir nicht, weil ich gar nicht kreativ bin!* (No, I don't like art, because I am not creative at all!)

Step 3: S–S

S1: *Gefällt dir Spanisch?* (Do you like Spanish?)

S2: *Ja, Spanisch gefällt mir, weil ich meinen Horizont erweitern möchte.* (Yes, I like Spanish, because I would like to broaden my horizons.)

5. The Hinge Question

A hinge question is a means of checking whether the students have understood the important concept in a lesson before we deepen the learning or move on to the next concept. Thus, the next steps in our teaching within a lesson hinge on how well our students have grasped what we have been trying to teach them. Hinge questions are targeted questions which are used at a strategic point in the lesson. How we as teachers respond to the outcomes of hinge questions may determine the subsequent pace and direction of the lesson.

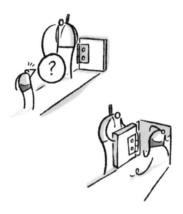

A good hinge question should be:

♦ Quick for the teacher to ask and easy for the teacher to evaluate responses – mini whiteboards are particularly useful in allowing the teacher to make quick judgements based on student responses.

♦ Quick for students to respond to – multiple-choice questions are often effective.

♦ Planned so that students will only get the answer right if they understand the key concept.

♦ Designed so that wrong responses may inform the teacher immediately of any misconceptions.

For example, a Year 12 lesson focusing on Spanish pronouns may contain the following hinge question:

Which of the following is the correct translation for 'I give the book to him'?

a. *Yo lo doy el libro.*

b. *Yo doy le el libro.*

c. *Yo le doy el libro.*

d. *Yo doy lo el libro.*

e. *Yo doy el libro le.*

f. *Yo doy el libro lo.*

Students who answer (a) do not have firm knowledge of Spanish pronouns, students who answer (b) and (e) do not have a significant grasp of pronoun positioning, and students who answer (d) and (f) have neither the accurate pronoun knowledge nor the awareness of positioning.

In her book *Making Good Progress?*, Daisy Christodoulou discusses how multiple-choice questions can be very precise and can focus on one aspect of a topic,[4] so they make good hinge questions. She goes on to explore why multiple-choice questions are criticised for being too simple because students can guess the answer. However, the way to mitigate against this risk is to ensure that there are a significant number of distractors – plausible but wrong answers – built into the multiple-choice question.

---

4   Christodoulou, *Making Good Progress?*, pp. 164–168.

6. Negotiating Meaning

The negotiation of meaning refers to a student's ability to work out what is being said to them in the target language through a process of checking and clarifying understanding. The ability of our students to figure out the meaning of linguistic input, and ideally to then manipulate it in the form of modified output, is a key skill for any language learner, even those who are somewhat proficient. I remember very well when, as a university student, I embarked on a year abroad in Germany and struggled with some initial interactions, including the verification of paperwork at the town hall and setting up a bank account, as well as health and dental checks. The ability to decipher meaning in circumstances which necessitated very specific terminology was crucial, and it involved me having to ask questions in the target language about the meaning of words, clarifying what certain phrases meant and rephrasing some of what was being said to me to check for understanding.

Interactions promote linguistic development in a number of ways, particularly those which include the negotiation of meaning:

♦ We learn from the language skills of our interlocutors by expanding our vocabulary and becoming aware of new structures and forms.

♦ We become conscious of gaps in our knowledge and, through the negotiation of meaning, bridge those gaps.

♦ We get feedback on our language use and modify it accordingly in order to make ourselves understood.

Creating opportunities in busy MFL lessons for students to negotiate meaning can be challenging. The pace may negate against it, or perhaps students may feel too reticent or embarrassed to try it. Additionally, the classroom contains lots of non-verbal cues – for example, if I use an intensifier such as 'lots' in my target language, I may subconsciously accompany it with a sweeping hand gesture so the students are aware of what it means.

If we are to offer our students opportunities to take real control of their language use, we must encourage them to develop the skill of checking and clarifying meaning in the target language, and foster (preferably spontaneous) chances for them to use negotiated meaning in the form of modified output. At A level standard, for example, alongside the set vocabulary we will teach our students, we will also want them to come across unfamiliar words and structures and confirm their meaning. This may be in the form of clarification strategies through quizzing and questioning in the target language, asking when something is not clear and paraphrasing accordingly.

It is certainly worthwhile endeavouring to promote an ethos in the MFL classroom of encouraging and celebrating the negotiation of meaning in the target language, even if it puts the pace of the lesson on hold for a few moments. For example, I find the GCSE photo cards used by some exam boards to be a good way to cultivate this approach. As part of their assessment, the students must describe what is in the picture. I ask the students to do this in pairs. We evaluate their efforts, and then I deconstruct a model description with them, which I have carefully pitched a level above what I think they are capable of. This will incorporate lexical items and structures which I know they won't have used themselves in anticipation that they will negotiate the meaning.

Let's imagine the picture is of a beach during the summer showing lots of families enjoying themselves. A typical deconstruction model, including negotiation of meaning in the target language, might go something like this:

T: *Hay familias en la playa – madres, padres y niños pequeños. El niño que está en primer plano, que está sonriendo, está jugando con un balón de playa.* (There are families on the beach – mothers, fathers and young children. The young boy in the foreground, who is smiling, is playing with a beach ball.)

S: *Perdone, no entiendo 'que está sonriendo'. ¿Puede explicar eso?* (Excuse me, I don't understand 'who is smiling'. Can you explain that?)

T: *Sí, está muy contento. Hay otras tres personas sonriendo en la foto. ¿Lo entiendes?* (Yes, he is very happy. Three other people are smiling in this picture. Do you understand?)

S: *Creo que sí.* (I think so.)

T: *¿Puedes decirme por qué crees que la chica que está al fondo está sonriendo?* (Can you tell me why you think the girl in the background is smiling?)

S: *La chica que está al fondo está sonriendo.* (The girl in the background is smiling.)

T: *¿Por qué está sonriendo?* (Why is she smiling?)

S: *Tiene un helado.* (She has an ice cream.)

T: *Bien. Para que quede claro, ¿cómo se dice 'sonriendo' en inglés?* (Good. Just to clarify, how do you say 'smiling' in English?)

It is also worth mentioning the effectiveness of online communication tools in the pursuit of high-level negotiation of meaning. If your school has access to a virtual learning environment with chat rooms, or if you use Google Forms or other such software, these have potential to develop our students' skills in this area and modify their output. This is perhaps particularly pertinent at A level, when our students hopefully have the maturity to use them wisely and maturely. These types of app have a number of benefits:

♦ There are no non-verbal cues so the students really do have to negotiate meaning.

♦ It allows teachers to structure the discussion/debate in the target language in a manner which is unaffected by the hurly-burly and rush of the classroom.

♦ All students have to participate.

♦ As the students are producing responses and negotiating meaning in a written format, we can set the criterion that they must modify their output following the negotiation of meaning. We can evidence this through their written outputs.

♦ They are perhaps more likely to negotiate meaning and modify their output in this less stressful environment.

♦ They can archive and return to the discussion at any time for the purposes of revision.

An example from an A level online asynchronous discussion may look something like this:

T: *Que'est-ce que tu penses du jeu vidéo* Fortnite*?* (What do you think of the game *Fortnite*?)

S: *Je l'aime et je le joue au moins trois fois par semaine. Je joue avec mes amis et ça m'aide à me détendre.* (I like it and play it at least three times per week. I play with my friends and it helps me to relax.)

T: *Est-ce que ce jeu vidéo a un effet néfaste sur les jeunes?* (Does it have a harmful effect on young people?)

S: *Je ne comprends pas – 'un effet néfaste'. Est-ce que vous pouvez expliquer?* (I don't understand 'harmful effect'. Can you explain this?)

T: *'Un effet néfaste'* – *un effet qui peut avoir des conséquences négatives, soit physiquement, soit mentalement.* (A harmful effect: this means it has negative consequences on people, whether physically or mentally.)

S: *D'accord. Certains gens trouvent que* Fortnite *peut avoir des effets néfastes sur les jeunes à cause de la violence.* (OK. Some people think that *Fortnite* has a harmful influence on people because of the violence.)

Reflective Questions

♦ Do you ensure that your questions involve as many students as possible?

♦ Do you 'cold call' to ensure all that students are thinking?

♦ Do you plan how students are exposed to high-frequency question words in your lessons from a very early stage in all skills – listening, speaking, reading and writing?

♦ What opportunities do you build in to give students the chance to formulate questions as well as answer them?

♦ Do you think about opportunities for your students to negotiate meaning in the target language by allowing them to question for the purpose of understanding and clarification?

Final Thoughts

This book has aimed to demonstrate how the six principles of great teaching and learning outlined in the original Making Every Lesson Count book might be applied within the context of modern foreign languages. It has endeavoured to demonstrate how current research in cognitive science may translate into the MFL classroom, while also acknowledging that there is a whole separate body of research into the science of second-language learning which may have implications for our approach. Underpinning the six principles are strategies for the development of listening, speaking, reading and writing skills in the target language.

This book does not aim to be a panacea, and nor does it claim to promote what an 'ideal' MFL lesson might look like. Teachers are, of course, best placed to decide for themselves which strategies they wish to adopt, amend for their own classrooms or indeed ignore. I would encourage all teachers to be discerning about what strategies they employ in their classrooms, based on a professional awareness and understanding of the context. Nevertheless, I hope that there might be something for everyone, whether they be senior leaders interested in the development of MFL within the curriculum, heads of department, classroom practitioners, newly qualified teachers, aspiring MFL teachers or those who have an interest in MFL education.

This book represents a snapshot in time – so it is inevitable that as the research develops, some aspects of lesson delivery espoused within these pages, and the strategies themselves, may need to be tweaked or revised. It is my firm view that it is an exciting time for educational research, and this is at its most exciting when research into cognitive science is married with research into second-language acquisition. When this happens, it has the potential to shed further light on effective classroom practice in the field of modern foreign languages.

While MFL in schools is undergoing a decline in student numbers, I have no doubt that social and economic realities, coupled with growing awareness and understanding of the science of learning and second-language acquisition, will lead to a revival in the number of students studying a second and third language. I am optimistic that our discipline has a bright future which will remain central to much curricular design.

It is my humble hope that this book might contribute in a small way to the discussion and debate regarding pedagogy. Like me, I'm sure you will agree that as teachers we learn every day. Some aspects of my teaching I get wrong and some I hopefully get right! I learn from many esteemed colleagues online and in my own professional working environment. Like a magpie, I collect many rich resources generously served up by other teachers. I hope that these pages have given a little flavour of what a privilege it is to teach MFL, the important position of our subject within the curriculum and the great benefits that language learning holds for our students.

Bibliography

Agarwal, Pooja, Henry Roediger, Mark McDaniel and Kathleen McDermott (2013). *How to Use Retrieval Practice to Improve Learning* (St Louis, MO: Washington University).

Allison, Shaun and Andy Tharby (2015). *Making Every Lesson Count: Six Principles to Support Great Teaching and Learning* (Carmarthen: Crown House Publishing).

Bauckham, Ian (2016). *Modern Foreign Languages Pedagogy Review: A Review of Modern Foreign Languages Teaching Practice in Key Stage 3 and Key Stage 4* (Teaching Schools Council). Available at: https://www.tscouncil.org.uk/wp-content/uploads/2016/12/MFL-Pedagogy-Review-Report-2.pdf.

Bjork, Robert and Elizabeth Bjork (2011). Making Things Hard on Yourself, But in a Good Way: Creating Desirable Difficulties to Enhance Learning. In Morton Gernsbacher, Richard Pew, Leaetta Hough and James Pomerantz (eds), *Psychology and the Real World: Essays Illustrating Fundamental Contributions to Society* (New York: Worth Publishers), pp. 56–64.

British Council (2017). *Languages for the Future: The Foreign Languages the United Kingdom Needs to Become a Truly Global Nation.* Available at: https://www.britishcouncil.org/sites/default/files/languages_for_the_future_2017.pdf.

Broady, Elspeth (2014). Foreign Language Teaching: Understanding Approaches, Making Choices. In Norbert Pachler and Ana Redondo (eds), *A Practical Guide to Teaching Foreign Languages in the Secondary School*, 2nd edn (Abingdon: Routledge), pp. 1–10.

Brown, Peter, Henry Roediger and Mark McDaniel (2014). *Make It Stick: The Science of Successful Learning* (Cambridge, MA: Harvard University Press).

Centre for Education Statistics and Evaluation (2017). *Cognitive Load Theory: Research That Teachers Really Need to Understand* (Sydney: NSW Department of Education). Available at: https://www.cese.nsw.gov.au//images/stories/PDF/cognitive-load-theory-VR_AA3.pdf.

Chambers, Gary (1999) *Motivating Language Learners* (Clevedon: Multilingual Matters).

Christodoulou, Daisy (2016). *Making Good Progress? The Future of Assessment for Learning* (Oxford: Oxford University Press).

Coe, Robert, Cesare Aloisi, Steve Higgins and Lee Elliot Major (2014). *What Makes Great Teaching? Review of the Underpinning Research* (London: Sutton Trust). Available at: https://www.suttontrust.com/research-paper/great-teaching.

Conti, Gianfranco and Steve Smith (2019) *Breaking the Sound Barrier: Teaching Language Learners How to Listen* [Kindle edn] (Authors).

Conti, Gianfranco (2015). How to Exploit the Full Learning Potential of an L2 Song in the Classroom, *The Language Gym* [blog] (15 June). Available at: https://gianfrancoconti.wordpress.com/2015/06/15/how-to-exploit-the-full-learning-potential-of-a-target-language-song-in-the-mfl-classroom.

Conti, Gianfranco (2017a). Eight Narrow Reading Techniques That Will Enhance Your Students' Vocabulary and Reading Skills, *The Language Gym* [blog] (22 July). Available at: https://gianfrancoconti.com/2017/07/22/eight-narrow-reading-techniques-that-will-enhance-your-students-vocabulary-and-reading-skills.

Conti, Gianfranco (2017b). Tempus Fugit: Four Strategies to Maximise MFL Curriculum Time, *The Language Gym* [blog] (29 July). Available at: https://gianfrancoconti.wordpress.com/2017/07/29/tempus-fugit-irreparabile-four-strategies-to-maximise-your-curriculum-time.

DeKeyser, Robert (2006). Skill Acquisition Theory. In Bill VanPatten and Jessica Williams (eds), *Theories in Second Language Acquisition: An Introduction* (Mahwah, NJ: Erlbaum), pp. 94–112.

Edemariam, Aida (2010). Who Still Wants to Learn Languages?, *The Guardian* (24 August). Available at: https://www.theguardian.com/education/2010/aug/24/who-still-wants-learn-languages.

Elliott, Victoria, Jo-Anne Baird, Therese Hopfenbeck, Jenni Ingram, Natalie Usher, Mae Zantout, Ian Thompson, James Richardson and Robbie Coleman (2016). *A Marked Improvement? A Review of the Evidence on Written Marking* (London: Education Endowment Foundation). Available at: https://educationendowmentfoundation.org.uk/public/files/Presentations/Publications/EEF_Marking_Review_April_2016.pdf.

Foreman-Peck, James and Yi Wang (2014). *The Costs to the UK of Language Deficiencies as a Barrier to UK Engagement in Exporting: A Report to UK Trade and Investment* (Cardiff: Cardiff Business School). Available at: https://www.gov.uk/government/publications/the-costs-to-the-uk-of-language-deficiencies-as-a-barrier-to-uk-engagement-in-exporting.

Graham, Suzanne (2014). Developing Speaking Skills in a Foreign Language. In Norbert Pachler and Ana Redondo (eds), *A Practical Guide to Teaching Foreign Languages in the Secondary School*, 2nd edn (Abingdon: Routledge), pp. 58–66.

Hattie, John (2009). *Visible Learning: A Synthesis of 800 Meta-Analyses Relating to Achievement* (New York: Routledge).

Krashen, Stephen (1982). *Principles and Practice in Second Language Acquisition* (Oxford: Pergamon Press). Available at: http://www.sdkrashen.com/content/books/principles_and_practice.pdf.

Krashen, Stephen (2004). The Case for Narrow Reading, *Language Magazine* 3(5): 17–19. Available at: http://www.sdkrashen.com/content/articles/2004_case_for_narrow_reading_lang_mag.pdf.

Kulik, James A. and Chen-Lin C. Kulik (1988). Timing of Feedback and Verbal Learning, *Review of Educational Research*, 58(1): 79–97.

le Carré, John (2017) Why We Should Learn German, *The Observer* (2 July). Available at: https://www.theguardian.com/education/2017/jul/02/why-we-should-learn-german-john-le-carre.

Lemov, Doug, Erica Woolway and Katie Yezzi (2018). *Practice Perfect: 42 Rules for Getting Better at Getting Better* (San Francisco, CA: Jossey-Bass).

Lund, Jess (2017) Aides-mémoire – 1. CUDDLES, *JLMFL* [blog] (15 January). Available at: https://jlmfl.wordpress.com/2017/01/15/aides-memoire-1-cuddles.

Mccrea, Peps (2017). *Memorable Teaching: Leveraging Memory to Build Deep and Durable Learning in the Classroom* (n.p.: CreateSpace).

Mitchell, Rosamond (2013). Making the Case for the Future of Languages. In Patricia Driscoll, Ernesto Macaro and Ann Swarbrick (eds), *Debates in Modern Languages Education* (Abingdon: Routledge), pp. 203–217.

Nuffield Foundation (2000). *Languages: The Next Generation. The Final Report and Recommendations of the Nuffield Languages Enquiry.* Available at: https://www.nuffieldfoundation.org/sites/default/files/languages_finalreport.pdf.

Nuthall, Graham (2007). *The Hidden Lives of Learners* (Wellington: New Zealand Council for Educational Research Press).

Pachler, Norbert and Ana Redondo (eds) (2014). *A Practical Guide to Teaching Foreign Languages in the Secondary School*, 2nd edn (Abingdon: Routledge).

Phipps, Wendy (1999). *Pairwork: Interaction in the Modern Languages Classroom* (Pathfinders Series) (London: CILT).

Rosenshine, Barak (2012). Principles of Instruction: Research-Based Strategies That All Teachers Should Know, *American Educator* 36(1): 12–19, 39. Available at: https://www.aft.org/sites/default/files/periodicals/Rosenshine.pdf.

Smith, Steve (2012). Pace, Challenge and Questions, *Language Teacher Toolkit* [blog] (25 July). Available at: http://frenchteachernet.blogspot.co.uk/2012/07/pace-challenge-and-questions.html.

Smith, Steve (2019). Single, Bilingual: What Do We Need to Know About Second-Language Learning? *researchED* (June). Available at: https://researched.org.uk/single-bilingual-what-do-we-need-to-know-about-second-language-learning.

Tharby, Andy (2018). *How to Explain Absolutely Anything to Absolutely Anyone: The Art and Science of Teacher Explanation* (Carmarthen: Crown House Publishing).

Waack, Sebastian (2018). Hattie Ranking: 252 Influences and Effect Sizes Related to Student Achievement, *Visible Learning* [blog]. Available at: http://visible-learning.org/hattie-ranking-influences-effect-sizes-learning-achievement.

Wiliam, Dylan (2011). *Embedded Formative Assessment* (Bloomington, IN: Solution Tree Press).

Wiliam, Dylan (2014). Is the Feedback You're Giving Students Helping or Hindering? *Dylan Wiliam Center* (29 November). Available at: https://www.dylanwiliamcenter.com/is-the-feedback-you-are-giving-students-helping-or-hindering.

Willingham, Daniel (2004). Practice Makes Perfect – But Only If You Practice Beyond the Point of Perfection, *American Educator* (spring). Available at: https://www.aft.org/periodical/american-educator/spring-2004/ask-cognitive-scientist.